D1517459

Budgeting Your Way to Financial Stability

LarsonAllen
Public Service Group

Budgeting Your Way to Financial Stability

Copyright © 2002 Larson, Allen, Weishair & Co., LLP. All rights reserved.

Authors: Debra L. Ruegg, Terry M. Fraser, Anne L. Howden, Susan Kenny Stevens

Design and production: Barbara Laun

Printed by: Ideal Printers, Inc., St. Paul, Minnesota

Edited by: White Fence Communications

Published by Larson, Allen, Weishair & Co., LLP, Minneapolis, Minnesota
Distributed by LarsonAllen Public Service Group
www.larsonallen.com/publicservice/
(612) 376-4500
(888) 529-2648

No part of this publication may be reproduced or transmitted in any form or by any means, electronic or mechanical, including photocopying, recording, or by any information storage and retrieval system, without the written permission of the authors.

This publication is designed to provide accurate and authoritative information in regard to the subject matter covered. It is sold, however, with the understanding that it is not intended either to offer or to be a substitute for legal, tax, or investment advice. If such advice or assistance is required, the services of a competent professional should be sought.

First Edition

Printed in the United States of America

ISBN 0-9652208-8-5
Library of Congress Control Number: 2002101692

Table of Contents

Foreword 5

Chapter 1

Introduction to Budgeting 7

    The Budget Defined 9

    Budgeting Facts and Fiction 9

    Relating the Budget to Financial Health 10

Chapter 2

Choosing a Budget Approach 13

    Line-Item Budgets 14

    Program-Based Budgets 16

    Income-Based Budgets 17

    Capital Budgets 22

Chapter 3

Preparing and Managing Successful Budgets 25

    Eight Basic Steps to Preparing a Successful Budget 26

    The Board's Role in Budget Preparation 30

    Management's Role in Budgeting 32

    Budgeting an Operating Surplus 33

    The Budget as Measuring Stick 33

    Taking Corrective Steps 35

Chapter 4

Budgeting Income 37

Support and Revenue 38

Conditional Promises to Give 39

Unrestricted, Temporarily Restricted, and
Permanently Restricted Income 40

Chapter 5

Understanding Your Costs 45

Fixed and Variable Costs 46

Defining Overhead 46

Covering Overhead Costs 47

Allocating Direct Expenses to Multiple Programs 49

Chapter 6

Building a Program-Based Operating Budget 51

Ten Steps to Developing Program-Based Budgets 52

Allocation Methods 68

Alternative Treatment of Fundraising Expenses 73

Chapter 7

The Budget and Pricing 79

The Concept of Unit Costs 81

Relating Unit Costs to Pricing 82

Chapter 8

Using the Budget to Create Cash Reserves 87

Surplus and Reserves. 88

Funding Depreciation 88

Budgeting for Reserves 90

Managing Reserve Funds. 92

The Board's Role in Monitoring Reserve Funds 93

Summary 95

Glossary of Selected Terms 97

Appendix of Worksheets 103

Worksheet 1: Income Projection Worksheet 105

Worksheet 2: Statement of Revenue and Expense with
        Budget Comparisons 106

Worksheet 3: Identifying Your Programs 107

Worksheet 4: Program-Based Budget. 108

Worksheet 5: Functional Time Estimate 109

Worksheet 6: Periodic Time Report. 110

Worksheet 7: Daily Time Report. 111

Worksheet 8: Salary Expenses 112

Index 113

Foreword

Budgeting is one financial subject every nonprofit knows something about.

Even with so many new and sophisticated financial models available today, the budget remains the financial tool nonprofits use most consistently to plan, monitor, and control both organizational and program futures.

Yet, as widespread as its overall application, few nonprofits use the budget to its fullest advantage. Even veteran nonprofit managers fail to get the full benefit from the budget's potential to cover overhead, to figure out unit costs, to improve fundraising plans, or to develop cash reserves. The budget can be used for all these purposes and more—and that's what this book is about.

We have written this book to tell you everything we've come to know about nonprofit budgeting over the past two decades.

This book is meant for small and mid-size nonprofit managers and board members who want to understand and strengthen their budgeting practices. We've organized it with the fundamentals up front and the more complex budgeting issues (overhead allocations, pricing, funding depreciation) in the later sections.

We've used plenty of examples throughout and provided you with timesaving worksheets to make your budgeting job easier. Worksheets for your use are provided both in Microsoft® Excel 97 PC format on the accompanying CD and in hard copy as appendices to the book.

Along the way, we'll introduce you to Hoops and Hope Learning Center, a nonprofit childcare and parent education program we created as a fictional reference for several budgeting concepts we'll present.

We dedicate this book to our nonprofit clients and readers whose ultimate financial success is measured by the good works they perform each year within available, but frequently limited, resources.

— *Debra L. Ruegg*   *St. Paul, Minnesota*
  Terry M. Fraser   *April 2002*
  Anne L. Howden
  Susan Kenny Stevens

Chapter 1

....

Introduction to Budgeting

Chapter Highlights

- The Budget Defined
- Budgeting Facts and Fiction
- Relating the Budget to Financial Health

Introduction to Budgeting

The budget is, far and away, the nonprofit industry's most commonly prepared and widely accepted financial instrument. Every year, in large institutions and small, millions of nonprofit managers, boards, and staff members undertake the process of preparing the annual budget.

Indeed the budgeting process, although universally dreaded, is among the most consistent nonprofit rituals. Yet today's shifting economic conditions in both funding patterns and cost escalation have made budget development anything but routine.

Historically, nonprofits learned to approach budgeting first from the expense side. Once expenses were formulated, they'd then tackle income projections, and with a few magical manipulations, produce the requisite balanced budget. Armed with the board's blessing, they'd go forth and spend, ever-hopeful that one way or another, there would be enough annual income to meet approved expenses.

But today's reality calls for a more considered approach to budgeting. As funds get tighter and competition stiffer, savvy nonprofits need solid financial know-how to adjust both to today's market realities and to ensure program sustainability.

Today, more than ever before, nonprofits are faced with a new level of scrutiny from taxpayers and other public funders. Likewise, many private foundations have refashioned their grantmaking to a "venture" and "outcome" approach. These new realities raise a whole host of questions nonprofits have rarely been asked before:

- What do each of your programs cost?
- How much does it cost to provide a unit of service?
- Which of your programs make money and which don't?
- How do your administrative expenses compare to program expenses?
- What percentage of your total expenses is fundraising?
- What is your organization's cost per dollar raised?

These are the types of operating and volume indicators today's nonprofits need to have at their fingertips to stay competitive for funds and ensure their firm grip on overall operations. The answers to these questions, and more, start with the budgeting process.

> **The budget is a nonprofit's annual financial plan that converts organizational goals and objectives into dollars and cents.**

The Budget Defined

What is a budget, anyway? In its simplest form, the budget is a nonprofit's annual financial plan that converts organizational goals and objectives into dollars and cents.

The nonprofit budget has two purposes:

> **1.** To *project* how much income can realistically be secured to meet expenses related to accomplishing this year's goals, and
>
> **2.** To *monitor* actual income and expense performance against what was projected, making changes in spending where necessary.

Many nonprofits think of the budget as a road map, their annual financial route to achieve the year's organizational goals and strategies. They make careful and considered calculations in preparing the annual plan and stick to it religiously.

Others view the budget as a straightjacket, a spoilsport that confines their creativity and potential. They slap the budget together at the beginning of the year and follow it until it no longer suits them.

No matter what your view or approach, at the end of the year, when you take stock of your annual performance, your organization's financial success or shortcomings will ultimately be a reflection of how well you composed, followed, and course corrected the budget.

Budgeting Facts and Fiction

Before going on, let's separate some budgeting facts from fiction.

1. *Nonprofits must have a balanced budget.* Yes, that's true. Your organization definitely needs to have enough income to cover its expenses. But it's also a good idea to incorporate small contingencies or surpluses into each year's budget, as a hedge against unrealized income and unanticipated expenses. It's even all right for your budget to be out of balance, as long as the overage favors the income side.

> **Too often we take the expense side of the budget as gospel, and the income side as a wish and a prayer.**

2 . *Once the budget is approved, it shouldn't be modified.* As a rule, this is true, but if circumstances change dramatically either positively or otherwise, the budget should be altered accordingly. If you were counting on a $100,000 grant, but received $50,000 instead, the expense side of your budget and corresponding spending will definitely need to change in mid-year.

3 . *We can't give staff raises because of the budget.* This may in fact be true, but who developed the budget and approved it? In some organizations the budget becomes the universal scapegoat for any management decisions likely to disappoint staff.

In truth, the budget is a set of financial goals, decisions, and priorities created by management and approved by the board. If salary increases or other items are not in the budget, it's because the people developing the budget didn't put them in, usually because of lack of funds.

4 . *If it's in the budget, I can spend it.* Not necessarily. If an item is in the budget as an expense, and income projections are on track, then this statement is indeed true. But too often we take the expense side of the budget as gospel, and the income side as a wish and a prayer. Important as the budget is, your organization's financial health depends on *income-based* spending rather than *budget-based* spending.

> *Income-based spending* refers to a practice of spending according to actual, rather than budgeted, income. It correlates to *income-based budgeting*, a practice of starting the budgeting process with realistic income projections and setting expenses accordingly. *Budget-based spending* refers to a practice of spending according to an approved expense budget, without taking into consideration any changes that may occur in the actual revenue received by the organization.

5 . *The budget has nothing to do with our financial health.* False. The budget has everything to do with an organization's financial health. Read on.

Relating the Budget to Financial Health

A few years ago a major national foundation asked us to work with one of its grantees, a superb and renowned arts organization led by a charismatic impresario known for pushing the artistic envelope in ways that both inspired and compelled audiences of all ages.

There was no doubt about this organization's artistic mission and values, nor about its ability to attract audiences at home or on tour. The problem was the nonprofit's historic inability to operate in a financially healthy manner. No matter how long or short their artistic season, no matter how large the audiences or successful the reviews, this organization lost money each and every year. So much so, that its accumulated operating losses were well over $200,000—more than 20 percent of annual operating expenses.

We've been at this work long enough to know that when a nonprofit shows these kinds of consistent operating losses, it generally points to a failure to make a connection between the budget they've prepared at the beginning of the year and the financial deficits they then must defend at year-end.

Financial health needs to be one of every nonprofit's goals. Without it, your nonprofit will spend the year scrambling for dollars rather than focused on more important items like clients, mission, and programs.

As we routinely tell our clients, *you may be "not-for-profit," but you're also "not-for-loss."*

The path to financial health is never an easy one, and indeed, it is certain to contain more obstacles for some nonprofits than for others.

But there is still one universal truth that, if followed, will assure a financially healthy condition for all. *Don't spend money you don't have*—and that all starts with proper budgeting.

> **You may be "not-for-profit," but you're also "not-for-loss."**

Chapter 2

Choosing a Budget Approach

Chapter Highlights

- Line-Item Budgets
- Program-Based Budgets
- Income-Based Budgets
- Capital Budgets

Choosing a Budget Approach

This chapter will present four approaches to budgeting you're likely to run into somewhere in your nonprofit career:

1. Line-item budgets
2. Program-based budgets
3. Income-based budgets
4. Capital budgets

Ranging from the simple, one-page, *line-item* budget to the more complex multiple-columned, activity-based format (*program-based* budget), each of these budget types presents a slightly different slant on how to project and monitor budgeted activity.

The first three budget types we'll discuss represent varying approaches to developing an *operating* budget—the projection of income and expense for program delivery and supporting services. You'll use the fourth type, a *capital* budget, in addition to your operating budget.

Knowing which operating budget format to choose is a judgement call that only you can make. But as a rule of thumb, if you are a fairly new organization that receives general purpose income from one revenue source, you can get by with a *line-item* budget. On the other hand, if your organization conducts multiple programs with varying costs associated with each, you'll want to pay attention to the *program-based* budgeting sections of this book, particularly Chapter 6.

Let's take a closer look at each budget type.

Line-Item Budgets

The *line-item* budget is a method of presenting an overall categorical picture of your agency's income and expense items. It gives you an at-a-glance look at what your expected income and expenses will be for a given period.

To see the *line-item* budget in action, we introduce you to *Hoops and Hope Learning Center*, a fictional nonprofit that will serve as our progressive illustration of several budgeting concepts. In all of the *Hoops and Hope* examples throughout this book, we will be looking at *operating* budgets without the inclusion of companion *capital* budgets.

Hoops and Hope started as a community-based after-school child-care program for first through sixth graders needing a safe place to spend time until their parents could get home from work.

Hoops and Hope soon became a stable part of the neighborhood's after-school childcare services. As it grew in reputation, parents began to ask for a summer program too.

By the end of its second operating year, *Hoops and Hope* had an operating budget of over $200,000, a steady enrollment of forty after-school students, a full-day summer program for thirty elementary age youngsters, and a new parent education program for which they had just received their first foundation grant.

Figure 1: **Hoops & Hope Learning Center**
Line-Item Budget

Income

Foundations	$ 25,000
Government Contracts	37,000
Parent Fees	159,000
Total Income	$ 221,000

Expenses

Salaries	$ 150,000
Payroll taxes	12,000
Benefits	14,495
Professional fees	7,000
Supplies	1,820
Telephone	2,100
Postage	936
Occupancy	16,750
Insurance	5,000
Travel	1,000
Depreciation	6,000
Total Expenses	$ 217,101
Excess Surplus/(Deficit)	$ 3,899

> The *line-item* budget is a method of presenting an overall categorical picture of your agency's income and expense items. It gives you an at-a-glance look at what your expected income and expenses will be for a given period.

While *Hoops and Hope* was a small, single after-school program, the *line-item* budget worked perfectly for them. But with the addition of two new programs, a more complex format was required. Enter the *program-based* budget.

Program-Based Budgets

Sometimes called a "functional" or "activity" budget, the *program-based* budget has two purposes. First, it isolates the activities of individual programs from one another. Second, it segregates program expenses from administrative or fundraising costs.

Program-based budgets have both income and expense classifications and are important for many reasons.

> Sometimes called a "functional" or "activity" budget, the *program-based* budget has two purposes. First, it isolates the activities of individual programs from one another. Second, it segregates program expenses from administrative or fundraising costs.

1. For the public, *program-based* budgets provide a mechanism to show that tax-exempt charities are meeting standards which are set and monitored by state and national "watchdog" organizations which require at least 70 percent of nonprofit income to be spent for program activities rather than fundraising or administrative activities. Note these are minimum standards. Our experience indicates that most nonprofits spend much more than 70 percent on programs, sometimes to the detriment of legitimate administrative expenses that would increase their organizational capacity.

2. The *program-based* approach to budgeting also provides a security blanket for foundations and other donors concerned that their *restricted grants* (donor contributions meant for a particular purpose or activity) are being correctly applied to the designated program and purpose, and not lumped into the overall agency funding pot.

3. Internally, the *program-based* budget gets right to the heart of each program's economic reality. On the income side, you can see exactly which programs have solid revenue sources, while getting a corresponding picture of each program's true costs on the expense side.

Understanding the economics of each program can be one of the most powerful tools a nonprofit board and management have at their disposal. Yet, over the years, we've seen some nonprofit managers who are reluctant to know what it costs to do business, particularly if they suspect that one program or another is losing money.

The truth is that in any multiple service organization, not all programs will perform equally. In fact, sometimes the programs closest to the heart of an agency's mission are most likely to lag behind financially.

The program-based approach lets nonprofits see the reality of each program's income and expense potential and compensate accordingly. This way, important programs that may not pull their weight financially may be balanced by others that overachieve.

Think of this as a *portfolio approach* to program budgeting. The key, of course, is to create a financial balance so that overall income and expense match in the total column.

Take a quick minute to review the *Hoops and Hope program-based* budget in Figure 2 (page 18), comparing it with their *line-item* budget shown in Figure 1 (page 15). Note how much more you learn about the organization in the *program-based* budget format.

We will have much more to say about *program-based* budgeting in later chapters, particularly in Chapter 6, which is devoted to the mechanics of this type of budgeting.

Income-Based Budgets

Traditionally, most nonprofits have learned to approach budget development starting with the expense side first. Then, only after expenses were formulated, would they begin to consider where income would come from to cover these expenses. And what if income projections fell short? Then, in the traditional budgeting mode, plans would be made to raise funds for the shortfall.

In this example (Figure 3 on page 19), *Hoops and Hope* has plugged its income gap with a projection of $17,750 in "other funding"—from sources yet to be determined.

Much of the time this system works, as long as suggested fundraising plans are both reasonable and expedient.

But if fundraising falls short, gets started too late in the year, or never quite materializes, then the *expense-based* budgeting method becomes a sure set-up for running an annual deficit.

> Sometimes programs closest to the heart of an agency's mission may lag behind financially. The *program-based* approach to budgeting lets you see the reality of each program's income and expense potential and compensate accordingly. It's a *portfolio approach* to budgeting.

	Total	After-School Program	Summer Program	Parent Education Program	Fundraising	Administrative
Income						
Foundations	$ 25,000	$ –	$ 3,000	$ 22,000	$ –	$ –
Government Contracts	37,000	31,250	5,750	–	–	–
Parent Fees	159,000	88,750	66,250	4,000	–	–
Total Income	$ 221,000	$ 120,000	$ 75,000	$ 26,000	$ –	$ –
Expenses						
Salaries	$ 150,000	$ 74,175	$ 54,935	$ 11,740	$ 950	$ 8,200
Payroll taxes	12,000	5,934	4,394	940	76	656
Benefits	14,495	7,168	5,308	1,135	91	793
Professional Fees	7,000	5,200	800	500	400	100
Supplies	1,820	900	500	260	–	160
Telephone	2,100	1,365	399	231	–	105
Postage	936	568	170	130	–	68
Occupancy	16,750	10,888	3,182	1,843	–	837
Insurance	5,000	3,250	950	550	–	250
Travel	1,000	700	–	300	–	–
Depreciation	6,000	3,900	1,140	660	–	300
Total Expenses	$ 217,101	$ 114,048	$ 71,778	$ 18,289	$ 1,517	$ 11,469
Excess Surplus/(Deficit)	$ 3,899	$ 5,952	$ 3,222	$ 7,711	$ (1,517)	$ (11,469)

Today, especially with funding patterns so rapidly changing, we suggest non-profits adopt an *income-based* approach to budgeting.

Whether your organization is supported by grants and contributions or earns its income through government contracts or program fees, the *income-based* approach will work for you.

As its name implies, *income-based* budgeting starts the budget process with income rather than expenses—and not just any income, but realistic, probable income.

Only when you've determined a realistic income budget will you have any sense of how much money is available to fund next year's activities.

This is a fundamental shift in thinking for most nonprofits, but one that, if adopted along with an *income-based* spending philosophy, will keep your nonprofit strong and healthy.

Figure 3: Hoops & Hope Learning Center
Traditional Expense-Based Approach to Nonprofit Budgeting

Expenses

Salaries, taxes, and benefits	$ 176,495
Occupancy	16,750
Other	23,856
Total Expenses	$ 217,101

Income

Secured Foundation Grants	$ 17,000
Government Contracts	31,250
Parent Fees	155,000
Other Funding	17,750
Total Income	$ 221,000

Excess Surplus/(Deficit)	$ 3,899

Figure 4 shows how *Hoops and Hope* prepared an *income-based* budget. You can see that it provides a further reality check by listing last year's actual income as a comparison to what *Hoops and Hope* is projecting for the current year.

Note the three separate income categories on Figure 4:

Certain	Income already received or committed and available to spend on next year's activities.
Reasonably Certain	Income fairly certain to be received that can be spent on next year's activities.
Uncertain/Possible	Income that has not been applied for, promised, received in the past, or has difficult conditions attached to it.

Depending on your own risk tolerance, you will base your budgeted expenses on either the *Certain* column only, or some portion of both the *Certain* and *Reasonably Certain* columns. No matter what your prior budgeting approach, be sure to resist the urge to base next year's expenses on *Uncertain/Possible* income. To do so is to risk coming up short at the end of the year, and will virtually guarantee an operating deficit.

As you can see in Figure 4, *Hoops and Hope* developed their proposed budget using the total of *Certain* and *Reasonably Certain* income ($221,000) and excluded income from *Uncertain/Possible* sources.

The *income-based* approach to budgeting should not in any way curtail your nonprofit's fundraising efforts or discourage your optimism. Indeed, where would the nonprofit industry be without optimistic leaders who set out each day to do the impossible?

Rather, what we're saying is this: Don't start spending money while it is still uncertain. Treat proposal income as a wish until it is confirmed.

Tough as this pill is to swallow, embracing the *income-based* approach, and then adjusting your expenses accordingly, will reduce the probability that your organization will spend or otherwise obligate money you're less than likely to receive—and this is what responsible budgeting is all about.

Continue to set your sights high. Develop as many fundraising proposals as you can to attract resources. Just don't start spending that money while it is still uncertain. Treat proposal income as a wish until it is confirmed.

	Projection to Current Year-End	Proposed Budget	Certain	Reasonably Certain	Uncertain/ Possible	Total
SUPPORT						
Government Grants						
1. County Grants	$ 22,000	$ 31,250	$ 31,250	$ –	$ 3,500	$ 34,750
2. State Grants	5,000	5,750	–	5,750	–	5,750
3.						
Foundation Grants						
1. ABC Foundation	3,000	11,000	3,000	8,000		11,000
2. DEF Foundation	10,000	14,000	14,000			14,000
3. GHI Foundation					5,000	5,000
4.						
5.						
6.						
7.						
8.						
Individual Contributions						
In-Kind Support						
Other						
1.						
2.						
3.						
REVENUE						
Contracts						
1.						
2.						
3.						
Earned Income						
1. Parent Fees	140,000	159,000	155,000	4,000	10,000	169,000
2.						
3.						
Membership Fee						
Interest						
Total Support & Revenue	$ 180,000	$ 221,000	$ 203,250	$ 17,750	$ 18,500	$ 239,500
			$221,000			

Capital Budgets

Nonprofits that own land, buildings, or significant equipment will require a *capital* budget in addition to their annual operating budget.

The *capital* budget outlines, frequently on a multi-year basis, the expenditures and corresponding income required to acquire or replace fixed assets or to keep them in good repair.

For smaller nonprofits with modest capital needs, there are two fundamental things to remember about budgeting capital items:

1. Capital purchases, such as land, buildings, furniture, and equipment, are assets that require their own budget and financial treatment. Unless these items are quite small (under $500 or below the threshold established by your organization's capital purchases policy), capital purchases should not be expensed through your operating budget.

   You'll need a separate budget for capital items, which means separate sources of income as well.

   Some nonprofits use annual or accumulated surpluses to cover capital purchases, while others undertake separate fundraising campaigns. Still others pay for capital costs through "funding depreciation," a concept we will explain in Chapter 8.

2. There is an important relationship between the *capital* budget and the annual operating budget. Since capital purchases don't flow through the financial statements as expenses, they are too often ignored at budget time. However, just like operating expenses, capital purchases require a defined source of income if organizational cash resources aren't to be depleted.

   Some of the toughest financial situations we see result when an otherwise solid nonprofit purchases a building but forgets to include, or inaccurately anticipates, the corresponding costs that will eventually affect the annual operating budget. Operating costs such as debt service, increased insurance, janitorial, utilities, and depreciation are examples of annual costs that spin-off from capital purchases and must be reckoned with in the annual operating budget.

> **The *capital* budget outlines, frequently on a multi-year basis, the expenditures and corresponding income required to acquire or replace fixed assets or to keep them in good repair.**

So there you have it. The four budget types your organization is either using now or getting ready to implement are: *line-item* budgets, *program-based* budgets, *income-based* budgets, and *capital* budgets.

With the exception of the *line-item* and *program-based (functional)* budgets, none of the other budgeting types are mutually exclusive. In fact, once your organization hits the size where the *line-item* budget no longer reflects your organizational activities, then you are ready to produce both an *income-based* and *program-based* budget for your operating needs, and a *capital* budget for your fixed asset necessities.

With these basic terms explained, let's start preparing the budget, the subject of Chapter 3.

Chapter 3

Preparing and Managing Successful Budgets

Chapter Highlights

- Eight Basic Steps to Preparing a Successful Budget
- The Board's Role in Budget Preparation
- Management's Role in Budgeting
- Budgeting an Operating Surplus
- The Budget as Measuring Stick
- Taking Corrective Steps

Preparing and Managing Successful Budgets

No matter which budget approach you choose, there are several basic prerequisites to preparing and successfully managing a nonprofit budget.

Eight Basic Steps to Preparing a Successful Budget

Step 1: *Plan your budget timeline*

The first prerequisite to successful budget preparation is solid planning. Depending on the size and complexity of your organization, you will need to start the budgeting process three to six months before the beginning of your agency's next *fiscal* year (your budget year). To calculate the right lead time for your organization, start with the date by which you want the annual budget to be approved by the board. The more board committees and staff your organization chooses to involve in the budget's development, review, and approval, the longer your lead time will need to be. (We'll discuss the pros and cons of participative budgeting later in this chapter.)

If you anticipate significant changes in organizational goals in the upcoming year (such as major increases or decreases in programming, the launch of a new initiative, or the addition of fixed assets), the budget timeline must provide for these. The calendar may need to be stretched, or other staff or outside experts involved, in order to develop budget estimates that accurately reflect the impact of these changes.

The remaining seven budget steps focus on preparation of the annual *operating* budget, though they could be applied to the development of companion *capital* budgets as well.

Hoops and Hope has a December 31st fiscal year-end and starts the budget process in mid-September to be ready for the new fiscal year. Take a moment to look at their budgeting timeline in Figure 5.

Step 2: *Identify organizational goals and priorities for the upcoming budget year*

The second prerequisite is to establish the organization's goals, priorities, and the program plans on which the budget will be based. Build a budget timeline that allows for solid discussion of next year's goals and program plans with the board and key management and staff.

September 17
Executive director sets budget timeline and communicates the timeline to key staff and board.

October 1
Executive director meets with key staff to discuss goals for next year.

October 11
Executive director reviews next year's goals with board at their monthly meeting.

October 12 through October 17
Executive director and key staff revise goals based on board input.

October 18 through October 26
Executive director develops a financial projection to end of current year and compares the projection to the current year's budget.

October 29 through November 12
Executive director develops first draft of income and expense budget, makes needed changes to balance expenses to available income, and develops written explanatory narrative.

November 15
Executive director reviews first budget draft with key staff and discusses the reasoning behind it.

November 19
Executive director reviews first budget draft with board treasurer.

November 26 through December 3
Executive director develops second budget draft, including revisions recommended by treasurer.

December 5
Board treasurer reviews second budget draft and recommends it to the full board for review.

December 7
Budget and explanatory narrative are included in pre-meeting board mailing.

December 13
Board reviews recommended budget for approval at their monthly meeting.

December 14
Executive director reviews approved budget with staff.

January 1
New budget is implemented.

Step 3: *Develop income and expense projections to the end of the current fiscal year*

The individual on staff who knows the most about the structure of income and expenses for your organization should take charge of this third step. Depending on the size and preferences of your organization, it might be the executive director alone or some combination of the executive director and financial, fundraising, and program staff. Using your most recent year-to-date income statement as a base, project income and expense totals from now until year-end.

Step 4: *Analyze budget-to-actual variances for the current fiscal year*

Using the year-end financial projections developed in Step 3, take a critical look at how accurately last year's budget matches projected actual performance. Try to account for differences (variances) between what you thought would happen and what actually occurred. The more you know about what went wrong and what worked, the better you will be able to budget for the future. If budgeting responsibilities are shared by department managers, be sure to get their input as part of this analysis too.

Step 5: *Budget income first*

Using the *income-based* budgeting principles introduced in Chapter 2, build your budget on realistic, probable income projections. Based on your variance analysis of this year's financial performance (Step 4) and the organizational goals you've developed for next year (Step 2), prepare an Income Projection Worksheet (Worksheet 1). This and other worksheets are provided both in Excel format on the accompanying CD and in hard copy as appendices to this book. For a sample completed worksheet, see Figure 4 (page 21).

Step 6: *Develop expense projections*

Determine which of your activities or costs from last year will not be repeated in the coming year, as well as any new or increased expenses that may be incurred to implement organizational goals. Take external financial realities, such as inflation or a tight labor market, into account. Then prepare either a *line-item* or a *program-based* projection of expenses for the coming year. (We'll show you how to prepare a *program-based* budget in Chapter 6.)

Eight steps to preparing a successful budget:

1. Plan your budget timeline
2. Identify organizational goals and priorities for the upcoming budget year
3. Develop income and expense projections to the end of the current fiscal year
4. Analyze budget-to-actual variances for the current fiscal year
5. Budget income first
6. Develop expense projections
7. Balance expenses to projected income
8. Secure board-approved budget before the new year begins

	Projection to Current Year-End	Proposed Budget	Certain	Reasonably Certain	Uncertain/ Possible	Total
SUPPORT						
Government Grants						
1.	$	$	$	$	$	$
2.						
3.						
Foundation Grants						
1.						
2.						
3.						
4.						
5.						
6.						
7.						
8.						
Individual Contributions						
In-Kind Support						
Other						
1.						
2.						
3.						
REVENUE						
Contracts						
1.						
2.						
3.						
Earned Income						
1.						
2.						
3.						
Membership Fee						
Interest						
Total Support & Revenue	$	$	$	$	$	$

The board's role in budgeting:
• Understanding and approving the annual budget before the start of the fiscal year
• Agreeing on fundraising role and following through
• Establishing fiscal policies for the organization's budgeting and spending
• Monitoring actual month-to-month financial performance relative to the budget and ensuring corrective action as needed

Step 7: *Balance expenses to projected income*

Now match your expense projections to your realistic income projections. Are your expenses "over" or "under"? If you have too many expenses and not enough income, cut expenses. You can always add them back in if you are successful earning or raising additional revenues. Remember that your goal is to have a balanced budget or better. This means that income should be realistically sufficient to cover expenses, with a little contingency or surplus to provide wiggle room.

Step 8: *Secure board-approved budget before the new year begins*

In the end, it is the board of directors who is legally responsible to ensure that your budget is fiscally sound and has been developed to further your organization's tax-exempt purpose. If you've developed your budget timeline wisely, all the necessary board committees and staff managers will have had sufficient opportunity for analysis and revision before the budget is sent to the full board for final review and approval. It's very important to have enough time built into the schedule so that the final budget is approved *before* the start of the new fiscal year.

The Board's Role in Budget Preparation

One of the board's most important roles is to understand the organization's budget and commit to it. If the board is expected to raise funds to make income projections work, be sure they are fully aware of this fact and are ready, willing, and able to accept the responsibility. Otherwise, you may be short of income during the year.

One of the all-time historical nonprofit debates centers around the board's role in fundraising. In our experience, there is no right or wrong answer to this perennial quandary. Generally, larger, more established boards do play a role in raising funds for the agency. But smaller or newer nonprofits, or those with a more grass-roots community focus, tend not to have boards with the same kind of access to money.

We have seen far too many examples of nonprofit managers who expect things out of their boards that are just not going to happen. Each organization will have to solve the board fundraising dilemma on its own. One thing is sure, though. The time to debate the board's role in fundraising is not during the budgeting process. Settle this point before the budgeting process begins, since you generally can't count on money to be raised by a board ambivalent about fundraising.

Would that as much time were spent on establishing board fiscal policies as on debating whether or not the board will raise money! Fiscal policies are something that, without any doubt, are a key responsibility of any nonprofit board.

Fiscal policies ensure that the budget reflects an organization's priorities and goals. They also establish the guidelines for both budgeting and spending. Some of the policies a board will typically establish are:

- Guidelines for annual board review of organizational goals and priorities
- Requirement for a balanced or surplus budget
- Requirement for a capital budget as companion to the annual operating budget
- Directives to operate so as to eliminate an accumulated operating deficit or build cash reserves
- Requirements for board approval of compensation, benefits, and personnel policies
- Thresholds requiring board involvement in decisions to create new programs, shift program focus, downsize programs, and/or significantly change administration, marketing, or fundraising structures
- Directives on the use of cash reserves
- Guidelines about the extent of budget revision the executive director can make without board approval
- Definition of the executive director's latitude in committing the organization to capital investments, leases, or contracts without board approval
- Requirements for board approval of capital projects and/or major fundraising efforts

In addition to policy-setting and annual budget review and approval, the board is also responsible for monitoring the organization's actual financial performance during the year, comparing this information to the budget and approving plans for any corrective action if the need arises. For this reason, it is essential that the board receives monthly financial information that is delivered promptly and presented with a budget-to-actual comparison.

We'll have more to say about comparing budget to actual performance later in this chapter.

The time to debate the board's role in fundraising is not during the budgeting process. You generally can't count on money to be raised by a board ambivalent about fundraising.

Management's Role in Budgeting

Management, too, has specific responsibilities in the budget development process. These include:

- Communicating the board's budgeting policies to others
- Setting a budget timeline that allows for input from appropriate staff managers and board committees, yet still ensures board approval before fiscal year-end
- Establishing the format for operating and capital budget requests
- Developing revenue and expense projections (possibly in conjunction with program managers and financial staff)
- Reviewing budget requests and making resource allocation decisions or recommendations to the board
- Presenting the proposed budget to the board, explaining its provisions and possible consequences

Second only in frequency to the board's role in fundraising is the question about how participative the budget process should be; in other words, how many people should be involved in the budgeting process, and to what extent? There are many schools of thought on this subject, with no one view more correct than another.

Our general advice is to do what works best for the culture of your organization. If you have department managers who dread budget development and would rather not participate in the process, then take your cue accordingly. If your managers are eager budget participants, then that's fine too.

One word of caution, though. Frequently, the executive director or development officer is responsible for projecting income, while department managers handle expense projections only. Hard feelings can quickly develop if realistic income expectations are not addressed early in the budgeting process. Be sure department managers understand the relationship between the expense budgets they manage and the income that covers those expenses. It is unfair to department managers to base expense projections on income that the executive director or development staff already know will be hard to raise. That's why we suggest the income-based approach to budgeting. It's better to approach the budget realistically than be told later about the need to cut back. You can always add expenses. It is much harder to cut back.

> It's better to approach the budget realistically than be told later about the need to cut back. You can always add expenses. It is much harder to cut back.

Budgeting an Operating Surplus

We shouldn't leave the budget preparation topic without discussing the role of *surplus* in budgeting.

In broad terms, the term *surplus* refers to the cash remaining once annual operating expenses have been subtracted from income. It's the money left over after all bills have been paid.

Operating surpluses are generated in two ways: 1) they are planned into the budget for the year; or 2) through a happy accident of fate, they just happen.

Some nonprofits are afraid to project a surplus for fear it will render them unfundable. Nonprofits with government grants in particular find surpluses hard to justify.

But the truth is that reasonable annual operating surpluses provide nonprofits with a cushion against unpredictable expenses and/or vacillating income sources. Surpluses give nonprofits more control over their own destiny and a jump start on the path to program and economic sustainability.

If you don't feel comfortable budgeting a surplus, then build a *contingency* line item into your annual operating budget. That way you can manage the unpredictable without going into the hole.

You'll find a further discussion of surplus and cash reserves in Chapter 7.

> **Surpluses give nonprofits more control over their own destiny and a jump start on the path to program and economic sustainability.**

The Budget as Measuring Stick

Up until now this chapter has concentrated on budget preparation. But the budget is also an important management tool for analyzing monthly progress toward annual financial and programmatic goals. Financial statements, when compared to the budgeted plan, help you assess whether your organization is really on track to achieve its agreed upon annual goals.

Figure 6 (page 34) shows how *Hoops and Hope* tracked actual operating income against budgeted projections in the mid-point of their last fiscal year. A blank worksheet in this format is also provided for your use at the end of this book in Worksheet 2 and on the accompanying CD.

	June			Year To-Date			Annual Budget
	Actual	Budget	Variance	Actual	Budget	Variance	
Income							
Foundations	$ 1,650	$ 1,600	$ 50	$ 12,500	$ 10,000	$ 2,500	$ 20,000
Government Contracts	3,000	2,500	500	18,000	15,000	3,000	30,000
Parent Fees	11,000	10,500	500	80,000	62,500	17,500	125,000
Total Income	$ 15,650	$ 14,600	$ 1,050	$ 110,500	$ 87,500	$ 23,000	$ 175,000
Expenses							
Salaries	$ 9,870	$ 10,000	$ (130)	$ 59,220	$ 60,000	$ (780)	$ 120,000
Payroll Taxes	780	800	(20)	4,680	4,800	(120)	9,600
Benefits	1,160	967	193	6,960	5,800	1,160	11,600
Total Personnel Expenses	$ 11,810	$ 11,767	$ 43	$ 70,860	$ 70,600	$ 260	$ 141,200
Professional Fees	300	340	(40)	1,800	2,000	(200)	4,000
Supplies	75	80	(5)	450	500	(50)	1,000
Telephone	90	100	(10)	540	600	(60)	1,200
Postage	60	70	(10)	360	400	(40)	800
Occupancy	1,120	1,120	–	6,720	7,500	(780)	15,000
Insurance	340	340	–	2,040	2,000	40	4,000
Travel	60	70	(10)	360	400	(40)	800
Depreciation	380	390	(10)	2,280	2,500	(220)	5,000
Total Expenses	$ 14,235	$ 14,277	$ (42)	$ 85,410	86,500	$ (1,090)	173,000
Excess Surplus/(Deficit)	$ 1,415	$ 323	$ 1,092	$ 25,090	$ 1,000	$ 24,090	$ 2,000

Although it is always a good idea to note significant variances to budget, sometimes nonprofit boards, and even funders, focus on a strict comparison of actual spending to the originally budgeted amount. In truth, the more important budget comparison, the one that will keep you out of financial trouble, is to compare actual income for the month to actual expenses. *Did we bring in enough money this month to cover expenses? If not, was there a sufficient carryover from previous months to cover expenses?* Deficits are caused by over-spending income, not by over-spending the budget.

Taking Corrective Steps

It goes without saying that for a nonprofit board or management to take corrective action when a budget goes wrong, timely financial statements are required that show actual monthly performance against budgeted expectations.

As simple as this sounds, nonprofits that get in over their heads financially generally share one or all of these three characteristics:

1. They haven't prepared realistic annual operating budgets, particularly on the income side;

2. They don't produce timely financial statements showing where they stand on a monthly or quarterly basis; and/or

3. They fail to take corrective action, preferring to bet on a long-shot income possibility rather than make operational cutbacks.

The process of taking corrective action when a budget goes awry is ultimately the measurement that separates *responsible* managers and *responsible* board members from those folks just filling a chair. *Anyone can manage when they have money. It takes responsible leadership to manage and govern when the financial chips are down.*

> **Anyone can manage when they have money. It takes responsible leadership to manage and govern when the financial chips are down.**

Chapter 4

Budgeting Income

Chapter Highlights

- Support and Revenue

- Conditional Promises to Give

- Unrestricted, Temporarily Restricted, and
  Permanently Restricted Income

Budgeting Income

As the section on *income-based* budgeting in Chapter 2 makes clear, only when a realistic income budget has been developed will you be able to determine how much money is available to fund next year's activities.

But making sense of what income can legitimately be included in the operating budget to meet next year's expenses has become more complicated since the Financial Accounting Standards Board (FASB) changed the rules about income recognition in 1994.

Support and Revenue

On the most fundamental level, nonprofit organizations have two types of income.

Support is money raised from outside donors, such as foundation grants, individual contributions, in-kind support, or any government grant that is given specifically as a contribution rather than on a contractual fee-for-service basis.

Revenue is income that is earned through service and contractual fees, box-office receipts, rental receipts, membership dues, or interest on investments and deposits.

Nonprofit Sources of Income

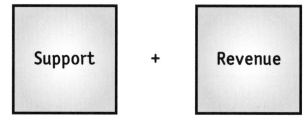

Support	**Revenue**

• Federal and state grants   • Government contract fees
• Foundation grants   • Earned income
• Individual contributions   • Membership fees
• In-kind support

Every nonprofit will have a different mix of support and revenue in its budget. However, it's always a good idea to diversify your sources of income as much as possible. If 70 percent of your income comes from three foundations, your organization is vulnerable to changes in those foundations' giving patterns. Similarly, if you receive 90 percent of your income from four government contracts, new government administrations with different policy or spending priorities could put a real crimp in your income prospects, and therefore your service capacity.

Your options for income diversification will directly relate to the nature of your organization's services and constituents. Some groups can limit their dependence on contributed income by charging fees for the services they provide, retailing educational materials or other products, or selling tickets to performances. Other organizations just don't have those options and seek to diversify income mix by broadening their base of government, corporate, foundation, and individual contributions. The key here is to work towards diversifying your income as much as you can. As traditional wisdom reminds us, "Don't put all your eggs in one basket."

Conditional Promises to Give

Since 1994, nonprofits have been required to differentiate between conditional contributions and those contributions without associated conditions. This is a very important differentiation to keep in mind when budgeting income.

1. A promise to give without any associated conditions is a "no strings attached" written or oral agreement to contribute cash or other assets to your organization.

   Most of the donations you receive for general operations, programs, and capital projects are unconditional. Although you are required to send the donor a report at the end of the grant period, as long as the agreed upon services or projects can reasonably be delivered, there is no question that the grant without conditions can be reported as income on your financial statements.

2. A conditional promise to give is different. In this case, the promised contribution won't actually be delivered unless some uncertain future event occurs. More simply, a conditional promise to give might not translate into actual income on your financial statements.

> **A promise to give without any associated conditions is a "no strings attached" written or oral agreement to contribute cash or other assets to your organization.**
>
> **A conditional promise to give is the written or oral agreement to contribute depending on the occurrence of a specified future uncertain event.**

A matching grant is an excellent example of a conditional promise to give. Before your organization can count on the income from this kind of commitment, you've got to raise the match.

Another example is a donor who promises a $60,000 grant ($20,000 per year) to support your food shelf program. Second and third installments are contingent upon proof that your entire agency has operated at a surplus the preceding year as evidenced by your annual audit. The condition here is that your organization must actually generate an annual surplus for two years in a row. Though you'll have the world's best intentions of accomplishing that objective, there's no guarantee it will actually happen. Only time will bring the required proof.

The budget impact when there are *conditions* attached to projected income is pretty straightforward. Conditional contributions should be *excluded* from the budget unless you're certain that the conditions can be fully satisfied during the budget year. For example, unless you're 100 percent certain you'll be able to raise all of the dollars needed to earn a full matching grant, it would be wise to exclude an appropriate portion of the matching grant from next year's income budget.

Unrestricted, Temporarily Restricted, and Permanently Restricted Income

This section is the most challenging we'll tackle as we sort out what types of income should be budgeted to meet next year's operating expenses.

Accounting standards require nonprofit organizations to classify their income into four categories: *unrestricted income*, *temporarily restricted income*, *income released from restriction*, and *permanently restricted income*. While these classifications involve a great deal of technical complexity, for our purposes we are going to focus on the budget implications only.

Let's take a closer look, then, at these four categories:

1. *Unrestricted income.* This includes all earned income, plus those contributions that have no donor-imposed restrictions, such as general operating support.

Contributions with some donor-imposed restrictions can be considered *unrestricted* as long as those restrictions don't prevent you from using the income in the upcoming year. For example, a contribution specifically restricted to a program you've been operating all along or that you intend to launch in the coming year should be included in the operating budget.

2. *Temporarily restricted income.* This type of income includes contributions with *donor-imposed* restrictions that preclude you from using the money as part of next year's operations. For example, the donor doesn't want the contribution spent until two years from now, or wants the money spent for an activity that your organization isn't going to undertake for at least another year.

3. *Income released from restriction.* These funds are the temporarily restricted income received in a prior period that can now be spent. "Temporarily restricted" means just what it says. Time passes, projects get underway, and income that was once restricted for a future year or purpose will ultimately be "released from restriction" and spendable. Though it may have once seemed quite far away, the third year of a multi-year grant does eventually arrive and income held aside for that year can be released from restriction and included in the upcoming operating budget. Or perhaps the terrific new program you raised money for two years ago is finally going to get underway next year. As a result, contributions that had been held aside for that program can be released from restriction and included in next year's operating budget.

4. *Permanently restricted income.* This category refers to contributions that your organization can't ever spend. The lion's share of such contributions are made to nonprofit endowments. Though the permanently restricted endowment itself is untouchable for operations, it does generate interest. If the donor did not stipulate otherwise, interest from permanently restricted assets is considered *unrestricted* and can be budgeted for use in meeting annual operating expenses.

So how can you put this information to work in developing your annual operating budget? Start by sorting all the income you think your organization will have next year into one of four categories.

1. *New income (contributed or earned) that can be used to meet expenses in the upcoming budget year.* This is unrestricted income.

2. *New contributed income that can't be used until some time in the future.* This is temporarily restricted income.

3. *Contributed income received previously and held aside that can be used in the upcoming operating budget.* This is income being released from restriction.

4. *New contributed income that can't ever be used.* This is permanently restricted income.

(Exclude all conditional income unless you're 100 percent sure that the attached conditions can be fully satisfied during the budget year.)

From these four categories, create your *income-based* budget using only the "unrestricted" and "released from restriction" income (categories 1 and 3 above). Any income from the second and fourth categories shouldn't be put into next year's operating budget. To include it risks two pitfalls:

1. You or your board could lose track of how much of the budgeted income is actually available to meet expenses this year, and the temporarily or permanently restricted income is mistakenly spent for something other than what the donor intended. The following year you'll be faced with an even tougher budget task—securing enough money to both meet annual operating expenses and replace the temporarily or permanently restricted income you spent by accident.

2. If you don't accidentally spend the temporarily or permanently restricted income you've included in the operating budget, by year's end you'll have an apparent operating surplus which creates the impression that your organization has a financial cushion in case of unexpected operating problems. In fact, the organization doesn't have a discretionary cushion at all. These funds are already committed for purposes intended by the donor. Again, you risk losing track of your real financial position and making judgement errors as a result.

The bottom line? Avoid putting temporarily or permanently restricted income into your operating budget, even if you anticipate that some of these types of income will be received during the budget year. Budget and report such income separately.

The bottom line? Avoid putting temporarily or permanently restricted income into your operating budget, even if you anticipate that some of these types of income will be received during the budget year. You should budget and report temporarily and permanently restricted income separately.

By using the techniques described in this chapter, you'll be better equipped to make sense of the various types of income your organization might receive in the upcoming budget year. Your objective is to develop an operating budget that includes only those certain or reasonably certain income sources *you are truly at liberty to spend in the upcoming year.*

Chapter 5

Understanding Your Costs

Chapter Highlights

- Fixed and Variable Costs
- Defining Overhead
- Covering Overhead Costs
- Allocating Direct Expenses to Multiple Programs

Understanding Your Costs

Budgeting is as much art as science. The process of accurately anticipating income and then realistically projecting expenses can be quite tricky, especially in a dynamic market economy.

This chapter will take a closer look at the cost side of nonprofit budgeting. It will step you through a framework for how to think about organizational costs, including a full discussion of "overhead," one of the most misunderstood and maligned costs of all.

Fixed and Variable Costs

One of the most basic distinctions you should make when budgeting costs is fixed vs. variable costs.

> *Fixed costs* are operating costs that do not change from year to year nor vary with an increase or decrease in activity. *Variable costs* are the opposite—they change in direct proportion to the amount of activity taking place.

Think for a minute about two expense items common to most nonprofits: rent and office supplies.

Let's say you've signed a five-year lease for $15 a square foot per year. This would be a *fixed cost* over the five-year period. Your office supply purchases, on the other hand, fall into the category of *variable costs*, since they "vary" from month to month.

When budgeting annual or future expenses, the rule of thumb is to keep fixed costs to a minimum. That way, especially if your organization is cash poor or has unpredictable and unstable revenue sources, you won't trap yourself with future obligations you can't meet.

Defining Overhead

The term "overhead" is the Rodney Dangerfield of financial concepts. It is consistently the most misunderstood term of all time. People use "overhead" to describe anything from bricks and mortar, lights and utilities, and management and administrative salary expenses.

On top of being misunderstood, "overhead," as a concept, is downright under-appreciated. In almost all circles its connotation is a negative one.

Nonprofit department managers resent it. Charities review councils want it kept to a minimum, and government and foundation funders don't want to pay for it.

Yet overhead is actually not such a bad thing at all. "Overhead" is the shorthand term for something more technically called "indirect" expenses.

Just as expenses can be classified as *fixed* or *variable*, so too can they be thought of as *direct* or *indirect*. While it may not seem immediately obvious, this is among the most important lessons of this book. Understand indirect expenses and you'll never again have to say, "I can't get my overhead or administrative costs funded."

A *direct expense* is one that can be applied specifically (but not necessarily exclusively) to a certain activity.

Let's say you are the executive director of an agency that has three programs. You've just hired a new teacher to work full-time in your English-as-a-Second-Language program. His salary is therefore considered a *direct expense*.

An *indirect expense*, on the other hand, is an expense that benefits multiple programs and can't be directly assigned specifically to one program or another. Common examples of indirect expenses are audit and accounting fees, general liability or directors and officers liability insurance, and general marketing expenses.

Let's take another example. If your organization prepares an annual report that recaps your agency's overall activities, this would be an *indirect expense*. The annual report benefits the agency as a whole. If, on the other hand, one of your programs prints a brochure specifically promoting its own services, then this program brochure would be a *direct expense* to that program.

Covering Overhead Costs

Now that you understand direct and indirect costs, let's use these concepts to figure out how to fully fund your budget.

Here is another story that is all too familiar.

> The term *overhead* is the Rodney Dangerfield of financial concepts. It is consistently the most misunderstood term of all time. On top of being misunderstood, "overhead," as a concept, is downright under-appreciated.

A few years ago we had a client that delivered social services to families and kids through five or six programs. Like many nonprofits, this group generated significant local project support for its individual programs. Still, money was always tight, particularly on the administrative side of the budget.

Early into our client relationship, the executive director called, ecstatic that the organization had just been awarded a $200,000 national grant for one of its childcare programs. This was the single largest grant the agency had ever received. The only disappointment was that the funder would only allow a five percent overhead allowance, just $10,000. So even with this new and sizable source of income, the grant barely put a dent in the organization's $100,000 general overhead expenses.

When we probed further, we found that the root of the problem was in the agency's definition of "overhead," as well as a lack of understanding of direct and indirect expenses.

Upon further review of the agency's $100,000 overhead number, we found many expenses that should have been classified as direct expenses of the childcare program, and thus would have been completely eligible for "program" rather than "overhead" funding.

This very smart and seasoned executive director, when asked to list his "program expenses," had counted *only* the salaries/benefits, classroom space, and specific activity costs generated by the childcare program in question. What he had not factored in was a portion of the gym, cafeteria, hallways, and even bathrooms these children would use daily. Nor had he included a portion of the accountant's time to do payroll or grant compliance reports for this program, nor the receptionist's time to answer this program's phones and greet its children and their families.

Instead, although each of these expenses had a clear and even measurable benefit to the childcare program, he'd classified them as "general/administrative," rather than program expenses.

Worse yet, the executive director knew he was eligible for even more than the $200,000 they'd received. He just hadn't been able to come up with additional program expenses, as he understood them.

> A *direct expense* is one that can be applied specifically (but not necessarily exclusively) to a certain activity.
>
> An *indirect expense* is an expense that benefits multiple programs and can't be directly assigned specifically to one program or another.
>
> Understand indirect expenses and you'll never again have to say, *"I can't get my overhead or administrative costs funded."*

Allocating Direct Expenses to Multiple Programs

It's easy to understand the allocation of a single expense to a specific program, such as the program brochure or English-as-a-Second-Language teacher examples mentioned previously.

It's a bit harder to allocate direct expenses to multiple programs. Yet understanding the rationale and framework for multiple program cost allocation is essential if you are to avoid the trap of minimizing direct costs.

Just because an expense can be divided among several program components does not make it "indirect." Many direct expenses (personnel, rent, utilities, janitorial, telephone, or supplies, to name only a few) typically need to be allocated among multiple programs. An expense is only "indirect" if the benefit of the expense *cannot* through a clear connection be assigned to one program or another.

Using the social services example above, if the day-care children used the gym, cafeteria, or lavatory facilities 35 percent of the time, then 35 percent of those direct costs should have been built into the childcare budget right along with the salary, classrooms, and other items used exclusively by the program.

Likewise, if the accountant spent 20 percent of his or her time working on activities specifically related to the childcare program, then 20 percent of that salary and benefits would qualify as a direct expense to the childcare program.

You'll see these principles in action and in much more detail in Chapter 6.

But for now, as we close this chapter, we hope we have convinced you that, in reality, most nonprofits have much less overhead than they think, particularly if they understand the difference between direct and indirect costs.

> **When budgeting expenses, keep fixed costs to a minimum. That way you won't trap yourself with future obligations you can't meet.**

Chapter 6

Building a Program-Based Operating Budget

Chapter Highlights

- Ten Steps to Developing Program-Based Budgets
- Allocation Methods
- Alternative Treatment of Fundraising Expenses

Building a Program-Based Operating Budget

This chapter will describe in step-by-step format how to put together a *program-based (functional) operating* budget. As we discussed in Chapter 2, a *program-based* budget isolates the activities of individual programs from one another, and segregates program expenses from administrative or fundraising costs.

To make things simpler, we've included worksheets throughout this section for you to complete. Extra copies of the same worksheets can also be found in the back of the book.

Since each of these worksheets requires several calculations, if you are proficient with spreadsheet software programs such as Excel or Lotus, you may want to spend the time setting up your own automated version of these worksheets, or use the spreadsheets on the CD that accompanies this workbook. The time you spend creating electronic templates will make your budgeting job easier both this year, and in years to come.

If you prefer the paper and pencil method, then find a calculator or adding machine (preferably one with a tape), a sharp pencil, and an eraser and you're ready to go.

Don't rush. Give yourself plenty of time to complete each of the worksheets. You will need it. But when you're done, you will have, in one place, a complete understanding of your organization's program income and costs, as well as the basis to conduct annual fundraising and to set program fees. More importantly, you and your board will have a full appreciation of the economics of each of your programs, and their interdependency on each other for covering shared costs.

Ten Steps to Developing Program-Based Budgets

Step 1: *Identify your programs*
Program-based budgeting starts with identifying your individual departments or programs. You may have only one program, or like *Hoops and Hope*, you may have three.

If this is the first time you've prepared a functional budget, program identification may be a little confusing. But generally, your activities will separate logically based on distinctions between types of clients served and types of programming. Keep in mind that not every organizational activity deserves the designation "program." For example, although a theater may conduct outreach programs at several schools during the year, each school served doesn't represent a separate program. All the school programs taken together would represent the theater's outreach education program.

In the *Hoops and Hope* case, after-school programming, delivered in a three-hour format nine months of the year, is quite different from the three-month, day-long summer program. Likewise, the quarterly parent education classes represent yet a third distinct program.

In addition to these mission-specific programs, *Hoops and Hope* lists "fundraising" and "administrative" as separate categories.

Take some time to look over the *Hoops and Hope* example in Figure 7 and identify your own programs using Worksheet 3 on page 54.

Figure 7: Identifying Hoops & Hope's Programs

Hoops and Hope's Programs

1. After-School
2. Summer
3. Parent Education
4. Fundraising
5. Administrative

Your Organization: _____

Your Programs:

1. _____

2. _____

3. _____

4. _____

5. _____

6. _____

7. _____

8. _____

9. Fundraising _____

10. Administrative _____

Step 2: *Assign program-specific income*

Now transfer your program categories from Worksheet 3 to Worksheet 4 on page 56, replacing "Program 1," etc., with your own program names. Modify the worksheet as necessary if you require more than the three program columns provided. Remember, these are available as Excel-based worksheets on the accompanying CD and as hard copies in the appendices to this book.

Using this worksheet, start filling in your income using these guidelines:

- First, assign *program-specific* contributions (new this year or released from restriction for use this year) and *program-specific* earned revenues to the appropriate program columns.

- Then place all remaining *unrestricted* income and income *released from restriction* directly into the Total Column 6 (A). You'll get a chance later to allocate this income to the desired columns.

- Now compare your total budgeted operating income to last year's actual amounts and sources. Is it reasonable compared to last year? If your budgeted income is more than the actual income from last year, are you being realistic? If your budget is less than last year's actual, did you forget something?

Resist the urge to allocate all unrestricted and released from restriction income now. It's better left until after you've prepared the expense budget.

Step 3: *Choose a method to allocate personnel costs*

Since salaries and related costs generally make up more than 60 percent of a nonprofit's expense budget, it's very important to make sure that staff costs are allocated to the appropriate department.

Allocating staff salaries to programs is simple if each of your staff work in just one program. For example, in a nursing home with two registered nurses, if one were assigned full-time to the rehab unit and the other exclusively to the terminally ill, 100 percent of each of their salaries would go to these two individual programs. But add a third nurse who floats between the two programs, and now you need a method to determine what percentage of his or her time belongs to which program.

		A	B	C	D	E	F
							Indirect
		Total	Program 1	Program 2	Program 3	Fundraising	Administrative
	Income						
1.	Grants	$	$	$	$	$	$
2.	Government Contracts						
3.	Fees						
4.	Interest						
5.	Miscellaneous						
6.	Total Income	$	$	$	$	$	$
	Expenses						
7.	Salaries	$	$	$	$	$	$
8.	Payroll Taxes						
9.	Health Benefits						
10.	Other Benefits						
11.	Total Personnel Expenses						
12.	Audit/Acct. Fees						
13.	Equipment Lease						
14.	Insurance						
15.	Training/Education – Staff						
16.	Promotional Expenses						
17.	Consultant Fees						
18.	Program Activities						
19.	Supplies						
20.	Office Equip./Repair						
21.	Postage						
22.	Telephone						
23.	Occupancy						
24.	Public Relations						
25.	Utilities						
26.	Depreciation						
27.	Other Supplies						
28.	**Total Direct Expenses before Indirect Allocation**						
29.	**Indirect Allocation**						
30.	**Total Expenses**						
31.	**Excess Surplus/(Deficit)**	$	$	$	$	$	$

To make that determination, you'll need to develop a system to capture where staff spend their time. This is generally accomplished through preparing timesheets or through a thoughtful time estimation process.

If the word "timesheet" makes you groan, you're not alone. But tedious as they may be, your program budget simply won't be accurate without a reasonably correct allocation of staff time. Note the word "reasonably." Nonprofits engaged in legal, accounting, counseling, or consulting services delivered "by the hour" will need to keep hourly time records so clients can be charged appropriately. And nonprofits receiving more than the legal threshold level of certain federal funds are required by the A-133, or Single Audit, rules to maintain hourly timesheets to verify funded program expenses. But many nonprofits can use one of the simpler models described below: *functional time estimates*, *periodic time reports*, or *daily time reports*.

- **Functional Time Estimates**
  The *functional time estimate* asks each staff person to anticipate or recall in which categories their time was or will be spent. These estimated percentages are then applied to the person's total salary and allocated on a salary worksheet, a process we will discuss later in this chapter.

  The *functional time estimate* (as illustrated in Figure 8 on page 58) is the least burdensome method for collecting time data. It is a good place to start, especially for nonprofits that have never before kept time records, and aren't particularly thrilled about starting now.

  The *functional time estimate's* major weakness is that it is just that, an estimate. Consequently it is only as good as the person's ability to project or recapture where they will or have spent their time.

- **Periodic Time Reports**
  Better yet is a time-tracking system that staff members complete at three or four pre-determined, representative times per year.

  Using this method, each employee notes time spent per program in the designated week, then turns their time report into the business office at week's end. These reports are averaged together to form the basis of each person's budgeted salary allocation.

Figure 8: **Hoops & Hope Learning Center**
Executive Director Functional Time Estimate

Staff Name and Position: Mary Jones, Executive Director

35%	After-School Program
35%	Summer Program
10%	Parent Education Program
5%	Fundraising
15%	Administrative

Using the *periodic time report* method as seen in Figure 9, we learn that the executive director actually spent 45 percent of her time in the after-school program, 35 percent in the summer program, ten percent in parent education, two percent on fundraising, and eight percent on general administrative activities. This is significantly different than what she'd estimated her time to be in Figure 8.

The *periodic time method* is a relatively simple and perfectly adequate time tracker for most nonprofits not required to maintain daily timesheets. See Worksheet 6 in the back of this workbook or on the accompanying CD for a blank periodic time report you can use.

• **Daily Time Reports**
Daily time reports are the most accurate method of tracking how staff use their time. Using this method, each employee is asked to keep a "real time" record of how they use their hours at work each day. These reports are not intended to track how many total hours an employee works each day, but rather to track how time worked was distributed among the organization's functional areas.

Executive Director – January 21 – 25, 20xx	Monday	Tuesday	Wednesday	Thursday	Friday	Total
After-School Program	6	1	3	4	4	18
Summer Program	2	3	1	3	3	12
Parent Education Program	–	3	2	–	1	6
Fundraising	–	1	–	–	–	1
Administrative	–	–	2	1	–	3
Total	8	8	8	8	8	40

Executive Director – May 20 – 24, 20xx	Monday	Tuesday	Wednesday	Thursday	Friday	Total
After-School Program	6	2	3	2	1	14
Summer Program	2	6	3	4	1	16
Parent Education Program	–	–	–	1	1	2
Fundraising	–	–	1	–	1	2
Administrative	–	–	1	1	4	6
Total	8	8	8	8	8	40

Executive Director – October 7 – 11, 20xx	Monday	Tuesday	Wednesday	Thursday	Friday	Total
After-School Program	4	7	4	5	2	22
Summer Program	2	–	3	3	6	14
Parent Education Program	2	1	1	–	–	4
Fundraising	–	–	–	–	–	–
Administrative	–	–	–	–	–	–
Total	8	8	8	8	8	40

Executive Director – Summary Total	After-School Program	Summer Program	Parent Education Program	Fundraising	Administrative	Total
January 21 – 25, 20xx	18	12	6	1	3	40
May 20 – 24, 20xx	14	16	2	2	6	40
October 7 – 11, 20xx	22	14	4	–	–	40
Total Hours	54	42	12	3	9	120
Percent of Time Spent on Programs, Fundraising & Administrative	45%	35%	10%	2%	8%	100%

Figure 10 records the executive director's daily time for January 16–31, as shown by the dates circled above each column.

Daily time reports can be used in a couple of ways. First, they can be used as a base for estimating employee time allocation for next year's budget, assuming programs and activities won't change significantly from the current year.

Another use of *daily time reports* is to total them on a monthly basis. These totals can then be compared with budgeted employee time allocations.

Although it has the potential to be the most accurate method for recording time, the *daily time report* can become a sore point in employee relations either due to the time required or a sense that management lacks trust in how employees use their time. That's why, unless you're required to use timesheets for business or compliance reasons, we favor the *periodic time reporting* method as a more all-purpose time reporting system.

You'll find a sample *daily time report* form for recording day-to-day time usage in Worksheet 7 at the end of this book and on the accompanying CD. This form can be used for either the first or second half of a month.

Step 4: *Complete the salary expenses worksheet*
Once you've chosen a method for capturing staff time, you are ready to complete Worksheet 8 (page 62), the Salary Expenses Worksheet. This worksheet will allow you to convert your staff time allocations into actual dollar amounts for your *program-based* budget.

Since this process can be fairly complicated, take a minute to look at *Hoops and Hope's* Salary Expenses Worksheet shown in Figure 11 (page 63). It will give you an idea of what your salary expenses worksheet will look like when you are finished.

- Begin by listing your organization's staff positions and the gross salary for each in the Total Column (A). List all salaries as 100 percent regardless of whether they are a part-time or full-time employee. On Figure 11, for instance, the bookkeeper is a part-time employee. The gross salary for this position ($4,400) represents 100 percent of that individual's time at the center.

Daily Time Report

EMPLOYEE: Executive Director   MONTH: (January 20xx)

DATE:	1 (16)	2 (17)	3 (18)	4 19	5 20	6 (21)	7 (22)	8 (23)	9 (24)	10 (25)	11 26	12 27	13 (28)	14 (29)	15 (30)	(31)	TOTAL
Program 1	1	0	1	0	0	6	1	3	4	4	0	0	0	1	0	1	22
Program 2	3	0	3	0	0	2	3	1	3	3	0	0	4	4	2	6	34
Program 3	1	4	2	0	0	0	3	2	0	1	0	0	1	2	6	0	22
Fundraising	1	0	1	0	0	0	1	0	0	0	0	0	1	1	0	0	5
Administrative	2	4	1	0	0	0	0	2	1	0	0	0	2	0	0	1	13
Sick	0	0	0	0	0	0	0	0	0	0	0	0	0	0	0	0	0
Vacation	0	0	0	0	0	0	0	0	0	0	0	0	0	0	0	0	0
Holiday	0	0	0	0	0	0	0	0	0	0	0	0	0	0	0	0	0
TOTAL	8	8	8	0	0	8	8	8	8	8	0	0	8	8	8	8	96

Worksheet 8: Salary Expenses

Position	A Total		B Program 1		C Program 2		D Program 3		E Indirect Fundraising		F Indirect Administrative	
	Percent	Dollars	Percent	Dollars	Percent	Dollars	Percent	Dollars	Percent	Dollars	Percent	Dollars
1.	100%	$	%	$	%	$	%	$	%	$	%	$
2.	100%	$	%	$	%	$	%	$	%	$	%	$
3.	100%	$	%	$	%	$	%	$	%	$	%	$
4.	100%	$	%	$	%	$	%	$	%	$	%	$
5.	100%	$	%	$	%	$	%	$	%	$	%	$
6.	100%	$	%	$	%	$	%	$	%	$	%	$
7.	100%	$	%	$	%	$	%	$	%	$	%	$
8.	100%	$	%	$	%	$	%	$	%	$	%	$
9.	100%	$	%	$	%	$	%	$	%	$	%	$
10.	100%	$	%	$	%	$	%	$	%	$	%	$
11.	100%	$	%	$	%	$	%	$	%	$	%	$
12.	100%	$	%	$	%	$	%	$	%	$	%	$
13. TOTAL	100%	$	%	$	%	$	%	$	%	$	%	$

Figure 11: Hoops and Hope Learning Center
Salary Expenses

		A		B		C		D		E		F	
		Total		After-School Program		Summary Program		Parent Education Program		Indirect			
										Fundraising		Administrative	
	Position	Percent	Dollar	Percent	Dollar	Percent	Dollar	Percent	Dollar	Percent	Dollar	Percent	Dollar
1.	Executive Director	100%	$ 47,500	45%	$ 21,375	35%	$ 16,625	10%	$ 4,750	2%	$ 950	8%	$ 3,800
2.	Lead Teacher	100%	32,700	50%	16,350	40%	13,080	10%	3,270				
3.	Assistant Teacher	100%	27,800	60%	16,680	40%	11,120						
4.	Aide	100%	19,000	60%	11,400	40%	7,600						
5.	Bookkeeper	100%	4,400									100%	4,400
6.	Secretary	100%	18,600	45%	8,370	35%	6,510	20%	3,720				
7.													
8.													
9.													
10.													
11.													
12.													
13.	TOTAL	100.0%	$ 150,000	49.5%	$ 74,175	36.6%	$ 54,935	7.8%	$ 11,740	0.6%	$ 950	5.5%	$ 8,200
													$ 9,150

- Next, add together all gross salaries noted in Total Column (A) and put the grand total on line 13 (A). You may need to modify this worksheet if you have more than 12 employees. For *Hoops and Hope*, total salary expense is $150,000.

- Then, using your chosen time allocation method, write down the percent time that each staff person spends in the program, fundraising, or administrative areas. As noted earlier, although several staff positions may be directly assignable to just one program category, others will need to be spread across two or more functions to accurately reflect time distributions. For instance, the lead teacher at *Hoops and Hope* spends time in three distinct program areas, while the bookkeeper is assigned to only one.

- Next, multiply the percent time that each staff person spends in each program category by their individual salaries. For instance, *Hoops and Hope's* executive director earns $47,500 annually. Since 45 percent of her time is spent in the after-school program, this represents $21,375 in costs to that program (.45 x $47,500 = $21,375).

- When the staff position salary allocations are complete, add each row across starting in column (B) to make sure that allocated salaries equal each individual's gross salary, and that individual percentages add up to create 100 percent. *Hoops and Hope's* aide position, for instance, was correctly calculated, since $11,400 + $7,600 = $19,000 and 60% + 40% = 100%.

- Then add each salary column down, putting the totals on line 13 (B)–(F). The total salary amount budgeted for *Hoops and Hope's* after-school program, for instance, is $74,175. You can now transfer each of these salary totals to the Salaries line (line 7) on Worksheet 4: Program-Based Budget (page 56).

You're almost through! There's just one more step, and that's to figure out the percentage of *total* organizational salaries allocated to each program.

- Using the Salary Expenses Worksheet (Worksheet 8, page 62) you've just completed, divide each functional area's total salaries by total organizational salaries shown on line 13 (A). This will give you the percentage of total organizational salaries for each functional area. *Hoops and Hope's* summer program, for instance, represents 36.6 percent of the organization's salary expense.

Enter these derived percentages next to the total salaries noted in columns 13 (B)-(F). This percentage distribution is known as "salary-weighted time."

When you have finished figuring what percentage of total organizational salaries belongs in each functional area, the sum of these percentages should equal 100 percent. Hang on to these percentages; you'll need them later.

Step 5: *Assign other direct and indirect costs*

Now that you've completed your Salary Expenses Worksheet and you've transferred the salary totals to line 7 on Worksheet 4: Program-Based Budget, you are ready to assign the rest of your costs across the functional areas.

- Using your own chart of accounts, or the expense categories shown in Worksheet 4: Program-Based Budget, project your line-item expenses, one-by-one, for the upcoming year and enter them in Total Column (A). Add them up and place the sum on line 28 marked "Total Direct Expenses before Indirect Allocation" in Total Column (A).

- Take a quick look up to the income totals and be sure now that there is enough overall income to cover overall expenses before allocation. If not, now is the time to shave off expenses. Be careful not to unrealistically pump up income at this point just to get things to balance. Remember that you have to live with this budget, not just prepare it.

- Next, allocate each expense line item to one or more of the functional categories you've listed across the top of the worksheet. To do this you will need to make a judgement about where each cost belongs. Here is also where the concept of direct and indirect costs, defined in Chapter 5, comes in.

  To make this allocation easier for you, the accompanying standard allocation method works for most small and mid-size nonprofits. Use it as a guide, knowing there will always be exceptions.

> **The fact is that none of your programs can function without the *indirect expenses* contained in your administrative and fundraising categories.**

Suggested Functional Allocation Methods

Assign these costs:	*By this method:*
Personnel Costs Payroll taxes Life/health insurance Workers compensation Disability insurance Retirement plans	*Allocate by salary-weighted time percentages*
Occupancy Costs Rent Utilities Maintenance Local telephone Equipment Leasehold improvements Business insurance	*Allocate by salary-weighted time percentage unless one program uses significantly more space than another. In that case allocate by square footage percentages.*
Direct Expenses	*Assign to the program they directly benefit*
Indirect Expenses Audit and accounting Legal fees Staff development Annual reports Board meeting expenses Subscriptions Agency dues/memberships Postage and delivery Equipment service/depreciation	*Assign to the ADMIN column except in cases where a direct assignment to one or more categories is in order.*

- Once you have assigned all operating expenses to one or more of the functional categories, add each line item across starting at column (B) to be sure the row total equals Total Column (A); then add expenses in each column (B)-(F) down. Put these totals on line 28 marked "Total Direct Expenses before Indirect Allocation" (B)-(F). These dollar amounts tell you the total direct expenses you've assigned to each of your programs and to fundraising and administrative.

- Just to be on the safe side, add all your "Total Direct Expenses before Indirect Allocation" items (B)-(F) across to be sure they equal the total in column (A).

Step 6: *Don't stop now!*

You should now have the expense side of your budget worksheet completed down through the "Total Direct Expenses before Indirect Allocation" total and program columns in row 28. (Yes, we know we haven't finished the income side of the worksheet yet. It's coming.)

Before moving on, take a moment to study your direct expenses. This is what each of these activities is projected to cost for the coming year if they could stand alone. And, indeed, this is where most nonprofits stop their budget preparation, content to know that, as is the case with *Hoops and Hope*, their after-school program will cost $114,048, the summer program, $71,778 and the parent education program $18,289 (see Figure 2, page 18).

But indeed, if you set earned or contributed income expectations based only on each program's direct expenses, you won't be able to cover your fundraising or administrative expenses. In essence, you will have shortchanged your income goals.

The fact is that none of your programs can function without the *indirect expenses* contained in your administrative and fundraising categories. So, the next step is to choose a method to fold these *indirect expenses* back into the various other program categories so you can establish each program's true costs.

Step 7: *Allocate fundraising and administrative expenses*

There are several ways to allocate your indirect costs (administrative and fundraising) to each of the programs, and we'll show you three sample methods here:

1. Percentage of total budget,

2. Percentage of salary, and

3. Percentage of client enrollment.

Each of these methods is perfectly legitimate. However, you need to choose the one that best reflects the way programs use administrative and fundraising services.

Keep in mind that the objective of this step is to find an indirect expense allocation method that balances efficiency with integrity, has a clear rationale, and is used consistently. In other words, you need a method that doesn't require so much accounting time as to be cost prohibitive, yet still best approximates the way administrative and fundraising services are used by each program. You are not seeking a method that simply helps each program to look good. You want one that lets board and staff more clearly understand the economic realities of your organization's program mix so that you can make policy and operating judgements accordingly.

The first step is to understand all three methods, and then start running your own numbers to see which allocation strategy best fits your organization.

Allocation Methods

Allocation Method #1:
Indirect Expenses as a Percentage of Total Budget Expenses
This is by far the most common and simplest allocation method. In this method all fundraising and administrative expenses are backed out of total expenses and reassigned to each program in proportion to the percentage of the organization's total program expense (not counting fundraising and administrative expense) that each program incurs.

An example will make this clearer. Lines 1 and 2 of Figure 12(a) summarize *Hoops and Hope's* budgeted revenues and expenses, before any indirect allocations.

Figure 12(a): Hoops and Hope Learning Center
Redistribution of Indirect Costs
as a Percentage of Budget

	A	B	C	D	E	F
					Indirect	
	Total	After-School Program	Summer Program	Parent Education Program	Fundraising	Administrative
1. Total Revenue	$ 221,000	$ 120,000	$ 75,000	$ 26,000	$ −	$ −
2. Total Expense before Indirect Allocation	$ 217,101	$ 114,048	$ 71,778	$ 18,289	$ 1,517	$ 11,469
3. Total Program Budget w/o Admin. and Fundraising	$ 204,115	$ 114,048	$ 71,778	$ 18,289	$ −	$ −
4. Program Budget as a % of Total Budget w/o Admin./Fundraising	100%	56%	35%	9%	0%	0%
5. $ Distribution of Fundraising to Programs	$ −	$ 849	$ 531	$ 137	$ (1,517)	$ −
6. $ Distribution of Administrative to Programs	$ −	$ 6,423	$ 4,014	$ 1,032	$ −	$ (11,469)
7. Total Program Costs	$ 217,101	$ 121,320	$ 76,323	$ 19,458	$ −	$ −
8. Program Surplus/(Deficit)	$ 3,899	$ (1,320)	$ (1,323)	$ 6,542	$ −	$ −

To arrive at each program's share of indirect expenses using this method, subtract fundraising ($1,517, column E (2)) and administrative ($11,469, column F (2)) from total expenses ($217,101, column A (2)). This yields a sub-total budget *without* fundraising and administrative costs of $204,115 (column A (3)). Then, divide each of the three program subtotals (columns 3 (B)-(D)) by the total in column A (3), which in this case is $204,115, to arrive at each program's prorata share of indirect expenses.

If *Hoops and Hope* used this method, 56 percent of the $12,986 fundraising and administrative total would be assigned to the after-school program (4 (B)), 35 percent to the summer program (4 (C)), and just nine percent to parent education (4 (D)).

Lines 7 and 8 of this chart show the adjusted program costs once indirect costs are fully loaded into the three program centers by adding lines 2, 5, and 6 in each column and subtracting from line 1.

Now look to see if, using this method, all three programs have revenues sufficient to cover the fully loaded program costs. You'll see that, although the parent education program more than covers its costs under this method, the other two programs don't.

Allocation Method #2:
Indirect Expenses as a Percentage of Salaries
Prorating fundraising and administrative expenses based on *salary* percentages is another common allocation method. The logic underlying this methodology is that, since the bulk of nonprofit activities revolve around how staff spend their time, it makes sense to reallocate indirect expenses according to salary.

So, to arrive at this percentage, we once again back out fundraising and administrative expenses from total expenses, this time reassigning the balance to each program in *proportion to staff salary percentages per program.*

Figure 12(b) shows this method in detail.

Lines 1 and 2 of Figure 12(b) again summarize *Hoops and Hope's* budgeted revenues and expenses, before any indirect allocations.

Figure 12(b): Hoops and Hope Learning Center
Redistribution of Indirect Costs
as a Percentage of Salaries

	A	B	C	D	Indirect E	Indirect F
	Total	After-School Program	Summer Program	Parent Education Program	Fundraising	Administrative
1. Total Revenue	$ 221,000	$ 120,000	$ 75,000	$ 26,000	$ -	$ -
2. Total Expense before Indirect Allocation	$ 217,101	$ 114,048	$ 71,778	$ 18,289	$ 1,517	$ 11,469
3. Total Program Salaries w/o Admin. and Fundraising	$ 140,850	$ 74,175	$ 54,935	$ 11,740	$ -	$ -
4. Program Salaries as a % of Total Salaries w/o Admin./Fundraising	100%	53%	39%	8%	0%	0%
5. $ Distribution of Fundraising to Programs	$ -	$ 804	$ 592	$ 121	$ (1,517)	$ -
6. $ Distribution of Administrative to Programs	$ -	$ 6,078	$ 4,473	$ 918	$ -	$ (11,469)
7. Total Program Costs	$ 217,101	$ 120,930	$ 76,843	$ 19,328	$ -	$ -
8. Program Surplus/(Deficit)	$ 3,899	$ (930)	$ (1,843)	$ 6,672	$ -	$ -

> **Nonprofit programs can't exist without administrative and fundraising expenses. So it only makes sense that we figure these expenses in when we think about true program costs. The method by which administrative and fundraising expenses get allocated to each program, however, should be chosen to reflect your best sense of how each program actually uses the services represented by indirect costs.**

Rather than use the proportionate program categories as the redistribution method, as in Allocation Method #1, this time we'll use the *percentage of staff time* devoted to each program as the allocation method. This is the same information you developed back in Step 4 for your organization on lines 13 (A)-(F) of the Salary Expenses Worksheet (Worksheet 8, page 62).

Using Figure 11 (page 63) from the *Hoops and Hope* example, we subtract $9,150 ($950 in fundraising and $8,200 in administrative salaries) from $150,000 (total salaries) to equal $140,850. Then, we divide each of the three program sub-totals by $140,850 to get its proportionate share of indirect expenses. (Lines 3 and 4 on Figure 12(b) demonstrate this calculation.)

Lines 7 and 8 of Figure 12(b) show what each program costs after indirect expenses are loaded back in using the percent of salary method. Add lines 2, 5, and 6 in each column and subtract from line 1 to calculate surplus or deficit for each program.

Once again, if *Hoops and Hope* chooses this allocation method, neither the after-school program nor the summer program cover their full costs. Only the parent education program runs a small surplus after full allocation of indirect costs.

Before presenting a third method, let's take a minute to restate a point made earlier, but easily forgotten with all the calculations we've made so far.

First of all, nonprofit programs can't exist without administrative and fundraising expenses. So it only makes sense that we figure these expenses in when we think about true program costs. The method by which administrative and fundraising expenses get allocated to each program, however, should be chosen to reflect your best sense of how each program actually uses the services represented by indirect costs.

The majority of nonprofits use one of the first two allocation methods listed above. But to illustrate how program economics can appear substantially different depending on the indirect cost allocation method used, we present a third strategy—and ultimately the one selected by *Hoops and Hope*.

<u>Allocation Method #3:</u>
Indirect Expenses as a Percentage of Client Enrollment
This method, although less broadly used, is predicated on the idea
that programs with the most clients use the largest share of the
indirect expenses, no matter what their budget or staff size. *Hoops
and Hope's* management prefers this method, a standard approach
in many social service agencies, because they believe it most faithful-
ly reflects what is actually driving program utilization of support
services.

Figure 12(c) (page 74) shows this method in action.

In this example, each of the program enrollment figures (line 3
(B)-(D)) are divided into the sum of the total fundraising ($1,517)
and administrative ($11,469) costs to arrive at the prorata percent-
age amount of $12,986 total each will be assigned. Lines 3 and 4
show this calculation. Lines 5 and 6 show the resulting amounts
redistributed to each program.

Line 7 presents the fully loaded costs of each of the three programs
and we can see that, under this indirect cost allocation method,
each of *Hoops and Hope's* programs has enough income to cover its
direct and indirect costs.

Figure 13 (page 75) shows *Hoops and Hope's* "fully loaded" *program-
based* budget using Allocation Method #3 (the agency's preferred
method) to redistribute and fully fund indirect overhead.

The three methods discussed above represent only some of the potential
strategies for allocating indirect costs. In the end, it's up to management to
choose the method that best reflects how programs utilize the organization's
indirect services and to apply the method consistently.

Alternative Treatment of Fundraising Expenses

Those of you with *program-based* budgeting experience will notice that the
allocation methods we suggest combine fundraising and administrative costs
together. There is an alternative method that appropriates enough unrestricted fundraising income to cover that category's direct costs, and then
allocates only the administrative costs to the programs. The rationale for

Figure 12(c): Hoops and Hope Learning Center
Redistribution of Indirect Costs
as a Percentage of Enrollment

		A	B	C	D	Indirect	
						E	F
		Total	After-School Program	Summer Program	Parent Education Program	Fundraising	Administrative
1.	Total Revenue	$ 221,000	$ 120,000	$ 75,000	$ 26,000	$ –	$ –
2.	Total Expense before Indirect Allocation	$ 217,101	$ 114,048	$ 71,778	$ 18,289	$ 1,517	$ 11,469
3.	Enrollment	170	40	30	100	–	–
4.	Program Enrollment as a % of Total Enrollment	100%	23%	18%	59%	0%	0%
5.	$ Distribution of Fundraising to Programs	$ –	$ 349	$ 273	$ 895	$ (1,517)	$ –
6.	$ Distribution of Administrative to Programs	$ –	$ 2,638	$ 2,064	$ 6,767	$ –	$ (11,469)
7.	Total Program Costs	$ 217,101	$ 117,035	$ 74,115	$ 25,951	$ –	$ –
8.	Program Surplus/(Deficit)	$ 3,899	$ 2,965	$ 885	$ 49	$ –	$ –

	A	B	C	D	E Indirect	F
	Total	After-School Program	Summer Program	Parent Education Program	Fundraising	Administrative
Income						
Foundations	$ 25,000	$ –	$ 3,000	$ 22,000	$ –	$ –
Government Contracts	37,000	31,250	5,750	–	–	–
Parent Fees	159,000	88,750	66,250	4,000	–	–
Total Income	$ 221,000	$ 120,000	$ 75,000	$ 26,000	$ –	$ –
Expenses						
Salaries *	$ 150,000	$ 74,175	$ 54,935	$ 11,740	$ 950	$ 8,200
Payroll taxes	12,000	5,934	4,394	940	76	656
Benefits	14,495	7,168	5,308	1,135	91	793
Professional Fees	7,000	5,200	800	500	400	100
Supplies	1,820	900	500	260	–	160
Telephone	2,100	1,365	399	231	–	105
Postage	936	568	170	130	–	68
Occupancy	16,750	10,888	3,182	1,843	–	837
Insurance	5,000	3,250	950	550	–	250
Travel	1,000	700	–	300	–	–
Depreciation	6,000	3,900	1,140	660	–	300
Total Expenses before Indirect Allocation	$ 217,101	$ 114,048	$ 71,778	$ 18,289	$ 1,517	$ 11,469
Fundraising to Programs Allocation	$ –	$ 349	$ 273	$ 895	$ (1,517)	$ –
Administrative to Programs Allocation	$ –	$ 2,638	$ 2,064	$ 6,767	$ –	$ (11,469)
Total Program Costs	$ 217,101	$ 117,035	$ 74,115	$ 25,951	$ –	$ –
Program Surplus	$ 3,899	$ 2,965	$ 885	$ 49	$ –	$ –
Total Clients per Program	170	40	30	100	0	0

* Program salaries are based upon Figure 11.

this approach is that though many governmental and philanthropic supporters are willing to fund some part of an organization's administrative "overhead," almost none will support fundraising. Therefore, a *program-based* budget that excludes allocation of fundraising expense is perceived by some as more broadly useful than one that includes it.

We have opted here to consider "fundraising" as an indirect expense analogous to administrative overhead and therefore include it in our allocations of indirect expenses to programs.

Step 8: *Allocate remaining income*

Our last step is to go back and allocate to the programs the "indirect income" (non-program-specific unrestricted income and non-program-specific income that's been released from restriction) you previously placed directly into Total Column (A) in Step 2. As with indirect costs, there are several different ways to allocate indirect operating income including Percentage of Total Budget Expenses, Percentage of Salaries, and Percentage of Client Enrollment—all described on the previous pages.

For consistency, you can simply use the same methodology you used to allocate indirect costs. But whatever method you choose, be sure you have a sensible rationale.

It's the proper job of management to decide what indirect income allocation method is the best choice for your organization. It's also a good idea to make sure that your board's financial leadership (ranging from the treasurer alone to all finance committee members, depending on the size of your organization) understands what allocation methods you are using for indirect costs and income and why you selected them.

In choosing an indirect income allocation method, look for an approach that can be applied consistently and reasonably across the programs. This will help avoid the trap of simply allocating the most income to those programs that are running the biggest deficits prior to allocation.

Step 9: *Analyze program economics and relationships*

Once you've completed the budget worksheet, be sure to take time to analyze the results of your work and share your observations with program managers and the board.

The *program-based* format can be quite revealing. It can tell you a lot about the economics of each of your programs, their interdependency on each other, and how the performance of each individual program affects financial outcomes overall.

If, as a result of using consistent and reasonable rationales for allocating indirect costs and income, some programs run a surplus and some a deficit, be prepared to discuss with your board why the deficit programs should appropriately be subsidized by the more profitable ones. Most reasonable people readily understand that, as long as restricted income is not being used inappropriately, certain individual programs are definitely worth continuing even if they can't cover their own direct and indirect costs. After all, your various programs comprise a portfolio you use to meet the diverse needs of your constituents.

Taken as a whole, however, financial reality dictates that your operations need to at least break even annually and, best case, generate a modest surplus that can be used as working capital for the organization overall. This means that the surplus generated by some programs after allocation of indirect income and expense has to be sufficient to cover the losses in other programs and still yield some net surplus overall.

By analyzing Figure 13 (page 75), here's what can be learned about the economics of the *Hoops and Hope Learning Center*:

- The nine-month after-school program is their most expensive program and requires a 26 percent government subsidy ($31,250 divided by $120,000 total income) to cover its total costs of $117,035. Nonetheless, there is still a small surplus, which gives the program a little wiggle room for unexpected expenses or fluctuating enrollment.

- The summer program is the second largest program monetarily and client-wise. But it has very little margin for error or added expenses. This program barely breaks even once all costs are loaded in.

- Each of these programs is completely dependent on the parent education program to make it work economically. By carrying a disproportionate share of the organization's overhead (due to the client enrollment allocation strategy), each of the other two programs is able to break even.

• However, the parent education program is funded almost exclusively by foundation grants, which can be quite transitory. It is imperative financially (and we assume programmatically) that this program stays funded. Because of its disproportionate administrative load, *Hoops and Hope* loses more than just a program if the parent education program is not re-funded.

Step 10: *Save your worksheets*

Congratulations! You've just completed one of the more complicated non-profit financial rituals. The first time is always the hardest. From here on out, it will be much easier.

Remember to save your worksheets, especially the salary expenses worksheet and your administrative salary rationale. You'll need them again next year. You'll also need them to set your program fees and prices, which is the subject of our next chapter.

---

10 Steps to Developing Program-Based Budgets

1. Identify your programs
2. Assign program-specific income
3. Choose a method to allocate personnel costs
4. Complete the salary expenses worksheet
5. Assign other direct and indirect costs
6. Don't stop now!
7. Allocate fundraising and administrative expenses
8. Allocate remaining income
9. Analyze program economics and relationships
10. Save your worksheets

Chapter 7

The Budget and Pricing

Chapter Highlights

- The Concept of Unit Costs
- Relating Unit Costs to Pricing

The Budget
and Pricing

Earlier in this book, we described the budget's fundamental purpose as a method to project and monitor annual income and expenses. Indeed, the prior six chapters have concentrated exclusively on various budgeting types, techniques, and philosophy.

But when properly approached and prepared, the operating budget can also produce further information critical to establishing program pricing and unit costs.

This chapter builds on the *program-based* budgeting methods presented in Chapter 6 and outlines how you can use the budget to establish your organization's per-client, per-day, or per-activity costs, otherwise known as *unit costs*.

The following story illustrates the importance of understanding costs from a unit perspective.

Several years ago an executive director came to us distraught that her agency, a women's shelter, which was solely funded by the local county, had lost $40,000 for the second year in a row.

The shelter had a maximum occupancy of 30 residents and received $39.90 per day for each, an amount the county considered generous, and our client felt "lucky" to have negotiated. Prior to this year, the shelter had existed on foundation support alone.

The director had brought along the shelter's most recent audit as well as operating budgets for the current and past fiscal years. The break-even budget for the prior year showed $436,905 in revenues and the same in expenses. Yet when compared with the audited income statement for the same period, the shelter had brought in only $390,800 in income, while spending at the full $436,000 level.

Digging a little further we realized that the executive director had used the following formula to set the budget:

$39.90 per day (x) 30 residents (x) 365 days = $436,905

In reality, although the shelter was in great demand, there were seldom 30 residents there at the same time. The average was more like 27 residents per day, which represented 90 percent occupancy.

The shelter had unwittingly established an occupancy rate of 100 percent and extrapolated it to an income budget of $436,905.

Working off more realistic occupancy experience, we came up with a number much closer to the $390,000 received in the prior year.

$39.90 per day (x) 30 residents (x) 90% occupancy (x) 365 days = $393,215

Now that we had solved the mystery of why the shelter lost money each year, the next question was what to do about it. Clearly the organization needed to do one of three things:

1. Reduce expenses by $43,000 and keep the per diem at $39.90 and the occupancy rate at 90 percent.

2. Renegotiate the $39.90 per diem so that expenses could be kept at $436,000, and occupancy at 90 percent. However, to accomplish this, the per diem would have to be raised to $44.33.

3. Create intake and discharge efficiencies so that the occupancy rate could come in closer to 100 percent.

Since the shelter was already partway into its current budget year, the second option, renegotiating the county contract, was impossible. However, the unit cost analysis had proved a real eye-opener for next year's operating budget and contract negotiations.

Using a combination of the first and third options, the shelter created operating efficiencies totaling $13,000 and raised the additional $30,000 from outside funders, ultimately breaking even that year for the first time since receiving county funding.

The following year, armed with the cost data we had developed together, the shelter was able to renegotiate its county contract to a more favorable occupancy allowance and slightly more favorable daily rate.

The Concept of Unit Costs

This is by no means an isolated example. And most nonprofits, particularly if they already do functional (*program-based*) budgeting, have most of the necessary tools to establish unit costs, or to check their current prices against true costs. They just don't know it.

Ask most nonprofit managers what their organization does and they can tell you in a minute. *We provide family counseling. We serve meals to the elderly. We provide musical instruction to at-risk neighborhood kids.* These are all "units of service."

Ask them further how many families they saw that year, or how many meals were served, or lessons given, and most could give you that number as well.

But ask the follow-up question, so much on the minds of taxpayers and state legislatures these days, and the information is less available. *How much does it cost your organization to counsel one family, to provide one meal, or give one lesson?*

Those who don't know, rather than admit it, will frequently answer this *cost* question with an answer about *price*. But in fact, as the shelter example so well describes, pricing and costs can be two very separate things.

Let's revisit *Hoops and Hope Learning Center* one last time to further illustrate our point. Note here that Figure 14 uses much of the information we saw in earlier samples, particularly Figure 13 (on page 75), but is adjusted to include unit cost (line 7) and pricing information (line 9).

Take a moment to review Figure 14, then read on to see more clearly the relationship between program unit costs and subsequent program pricing.

Relating Unit Costs to Pricing

For many commercial businesses, pricing a product or a unit of service is sometimes as simple as adding up all the associated costs and then applying a desirable profit margin. And though businesses have their own struggles with decisions about price points, short selling cycles, and discounting, their main focus is always on two things: generating both sufficient sales volume and profit so the company can thrive and grow.

In the nonprofit marketplace, we are less concerned about profit (although a little surplus is always a good thing), and more concerned about keeping our prices low enough to be affordable.

As tax-exempt entities, nonprofits have an advantage most businesses don't. We have *the potential for foundation and government subsidies.* In addition to helping nonprofits achieve their mission and program purposes, private and

Figure 14: Hoops and Hope Learning Center
Program Budget with Student Enrollment

	Total	After-School Program	Summer Program	Parent Education Program	Indirect Fundraising	Administrative
1. Enrollment	# 170	# 40	# 30	# 100		
2. Total Revenue	$ 221,000	$ 120,000	$ 75,000	$ 26,000	$ –	$ –
3. Total Expense before Indirect Allocation	$ 217,101	$ 114,048	$ 71,778	$ 18,289	$ 1,517	$ 11,469
4. $ Distribution of Fundraising and Admin. to Programs	$ –	$ 2,987	$ 2,337	$ 7,662	$ (1,517)	$ (11,469)
5. Total Program Costs	$ 217,101	$ 117,035	$ 74,115	$ 25,951	$ –	$ –
6. Program Surplus (Deficit)	$ 3,899	$ 2,965	$ 885	$ 49	$ –	$ –
7. Annual Per Participant Cost		$ 2,925.88	$ 2,470.50	$ 259.51		
8. Weekly Unit Cost per Participant		$ 73.15	$ 205.88	$ 28.83		
9. Subsidized Cost per Participant		19.53/wk	24.31/wk	220.00/qtr		
10. Price per Participant		55.50/wk	184.03/wk	40.00/qtr		

After School: x 40 week program
Summer: x 12 week program
Parent Education: x 9 weeks, 4 times a year

> As tax-exempt entities, nonprofits have an advantage most businesses don't. We have the potential for foundation and government subsidies. In addition to helping nonprofits achieve their mission and program purposes, private and public subsidies have the financial effect of offsetting a nonprofit's true costs, and thus making services more affordable and accessible to the community.

public subsidies have the financial effect of offsetting a nonprofit's true costs, and thus making services more affordable and accessible to the community.

When these subsidies are taken for granted or not fully understood, it becomes easy to delude ourselves that price and costs are identical concepts in donor-supported nonprofits. This is seldom, if ever, true.

So how can nonprofits strategically use cost data to set prices? Let's see how *Hoops and Hope* did it with each of their three programs.

- **The After-School Program's Unit Costs and Pricing Structure**
  We'll start with the after-school program with its enrollment of 40 students and expense budget of $117,035. The dividend of these two numbers ($2,926) provides this program's overall per-student cost. But since this program is conducted on a weekly basis, these numbers need to be taken a step further.

  Hoops and Hope's after-school program follows the 40-week school year and receives payment by the week for 40 kids. To determine the after-school program's weekly cost per student, we'd use the following formula:

  $117,035 (÷) 40 students (÷) 40 weeks = $73.15 per student per week.

  It costs *Hoops and Hope* $73.15 per week per child to provide the after-school program. But what do they charge parents?

  The weekly cost to parents is $55.50. A government grant of $31,250 subsidizes the approximately $19.50 per student weekly difference.

  $31,250 (÷) 40 students (÷) 40 weeks = $19.53 per student per week

- **The Summer Program's Unit Costs and Pricing Structure**
  The calculations for coming up with the summer program's unit costs are much the same.

  This is a 12-week program anticipated to be fully subscribed with a maximum of 30 students. The *per-student cost* of $2,471 is derived by dividing total program costs ($74,115) by the number of students (30).

The *cost per week* is then calculated by dividing the per-student cost by the program's 12 weeks to reach a weekly cost per student of approximately $206.

But because *Hoops and Hope* receives an $8,750 government and foundation subsidy for this program, they are able to discount this weekly fee to $184 using the following calculation.

$75,000 (-) $8,750 (÷) 30 students (÷) 12 weeks = $184.03

$206 per week then is their *cost*, but because of the foundation/government subsidy, the program's *price* can be set at $184.03

- **The Parent Education Program's Unit Costs and Pricing Structure**
  The prior two examples have assumed a fully subscribed maximum occupancy. *Hoops and Hope's* parent education program is another story.

  This program is offered quarterly, in nine-week sessions, and though it is held in a classroom capable of holding 50 adults comfortably, enrollment has never exceeded 25.

  We know that the total cost of this program is $25,951, and the average annual enrollment is 100 (25 per quarter).

  Simple costing would say that *Hoops and Hope* spends $260 per parent per quarter to instruct each parent, or about $29 per week (for the nine-week session) for each parent attending.

  $25,951 (÷) 100 parents (÷) 9 weeks = $28.83 per week per parent

  But this example, even more than the others, brings home the significant differences between cost and price. There is no way that *Hoops and Hope's* parents can pay $29 a week to attend parent education classes. So *Hoops and Hope* wisely has negotiated a foundation grant to supplement minimal parent fees.

  Now instead of the $260 costs for a nine-week program, *Hoops and Hope* is able to charge parents a quarterly program fee of only $40. The rest is subsidized by the foundation grant.

  $25,951 total costs (-) $22,000 foundation grant (÷) 25 parents (÷) 4 quarters = $39.51 per parent per quarter.

We hope these examples, detailed as they are, have provided a framework for you to think about your nonprofit's unit costs and prices. The logic underlying these examples can be applied to many different types of programs—from theatrical productions to member services.

And though the subject of both costs and price are nearly inexhaustible topics, the fundamental point to remember is this: Know and understand your unit costs before setting your price.

And what's the undergirding framework for understanding your costs? The *program-based* budget!

Chapter 8

···

Using the Budget to Create Cash Reserves

Chapter Highlights

• Surplus and Reserves

• Funding Depreciation

• Budgeting for Reserves

• Managing Reserve Funds

• The Board's Role in Monitoring Reserve Funds

Using the Budget to Create Cash Reserves

Throughout this book we've talked about the important role surpluses play in maintaining a strong and healthy nonprofit organization.

This chapter discusses *cash reserves*, a somewhat "glorified" surplus, and, more specifically, how strategic budgeting techniques can help you create surpluses and cash reserves for your organization.

Surplus and Reserves

Let's start by defining two terms that are frequently, but mistakenly, used synonymously: *surplus* and *reserves*.

> *Surplus* refers to the cash that remains at the end of a period once all expenses have been subtracted from income.
>
> *Reserves* are surpluses that have been strategically set aside by the board or management for designated purposes. These purposes might be operating in nature, hence the term "cash reserve" or "operating reserve." They may also be designated for fixed asset replacement, sometimes also called "repair and replacement" reserves.

Either way, reserve funds provide nonprofits with an extra level of financial security and should be a standard part of any mid-size organization's financial portfolio.

Funding Depreciation

Any nonprofit with *fixed assets* (buildings, furnishings, or equipment) can produce automatic annual cash surpluses by simply including a line item for "depreciation" in their operating budget.

Depreciation is a non-cash expense that recognizes the declining value of an asset. However, your organization doesn't actually pay out any cash to cover it. We include depreciation in the annual budget to "match" the expense of the capital asset with the revenue it generates. When you achieve enough income to fund all expenses, at the end of the year you'll have generated excess cash to the tune of that year's budgeted depreciation amount.

Need more explanation? Maybe this will help:

Any time your organization buys a new piece of equipment, the value of the purchase is recorded at market price in the year purchased. That original price is then depreciated over a given period of time (known as its "useful life") to reflect its declining value. The declining value is recorded on a depreciation schedule that is used to create the fixed asset value on the audited statement's balance sheet.

Here's an example.

Figure 15: Sample Depreciation Schedule

Purchase Date	Description	Cost	Useful-Life	2003 Depreciation	2004 Depreciation	2005 Depreciation
December, 2002	Computer	$1,800	3 years	$600	$600	$600

Let's say you bought a computer in 2002 for $1,800 and it has a useful life of three years. In the annual audit for 2002, the net value of that item on your balance sheet will be reflected as $1,800. In 2003, its value will be $1,200; and in 2004, $600; and by 2005, it will be fully depreciated down to $0, whether or not it is still in use.

The annual declining value, in this case $600 per year, is that year's depreciation amount.

If that computer was the only fixed asset your organization owned, the depreciation expense you'd be entitled to bring into each of those years' budgets would be $600 per year.

If you were to take the extra step to build this $600 item into your operating budget, *and* if you receive enough income to cover all cash expenses plus the depreciation, then technically, you'd have $600 that, although budgeted as an expense, wasn't paid out that year to purchase anything.

Your budget will balance to $0, but there is actually an extra $600 in cash that's been generated by your operations for the year. On the balance sheet, this is reflected as an increase in cash and a decrease of $600 in fixed asset

Fixed Asset
An asset that has a relatively long useful life, usually several years or more, such as land, buildings, and equipment.

Depreciation
The process by which the cost of a fixed asset is expensed over its useful life.

value. By covering the depreciating value of your fixed assets (the computer) with cash income you've "funded depreciation." Take a moment to review the example in Figure 16 on page 91.

Budgeting for Reserves
Now let's look at one more example, this time from a larger organization.

Figure 17 presents an abbreviated statement of budgeted income and expense compared to actual financial statement performance for a mid-size nonprofit.

Figure 17: Sample Budget with Depreciation
Compared to Actual Revenues and Expenses

	Projected Budget	Actual Performance
Income		
Support	$ 500,000	$ 400,000
Revenue	900,000	730,000
Total	$ 1,400,000	$ 1,130,000
Expenses		
Program	$ 1,100,000	$ 910,000
Administrative	150,000	100,000
Fundraising	125,000	95,000
Depreciation	25,000	25,000
Total	$ 1,400,000	$ 1,130,000

Column 1 of the example shows depreciation projected at $25,000 in the expense categories. In column 2 you'll see that, although the organization failed to meet its budgeted income projections, by decreasing costs accordingly, it still broke even, and even managed to cover its depreciation at the same time.

If this nonprofit now takes the $25,000 budgeted for depreciation out of its operating net assets and sets it aside in a savings account of some sort, then it will not only have funded depreciation, but established a savings reserve as well.

Figure 16: Sample Balance Sheet and Income Statement

Income Statement

Income		
Support	$	50,000
Revenue		100,000
Total income		$ 150,000
Expenses		
Program	$	125,000
Administrative		20,000
Fundraising		4,400
Depreciation		600
Total expenses		$ 150,000

Balance Sheet with Cash Reserve

Current Assets		
Cash – checking	$	2,000
Cash – reserve		600
Total current assets		$ 2,600
Property and Equipment		
Equipment		1,800
Accumulated depreciation		(600)
Total property and equipment		$ 1,200
Total Assets		$ 3,800
Current Liabilities		
Accounts payable	$	1,000
Total current liabilities		$ 1,000
Unrestricted Net Assets		
Undesignated net assets	$	2,200
Board designated cash reserve		600
Total unrestricted net assets		$ 2,800
Total Liabilities and Net Assets		$ 3,800

But remember, this technique only works if you've generated enough income to cover all expenses, including depreciation. Once nonprofits see the advantage to this technique, we are frequently asked *how much depreciation can I build into my annual budget?*

The simple answer is that you can bring into your budget only an amount up to the figure on your organization's capital asset depreciation schedule.

In reality, though, you'll need to use judgement about how much of the depreciation in your annual budget you can realistically plan to fund, particularly if your organization has a large depreciation number. To "fund" depreciation, you need to generate enough income to cover the depreciation "expense" as well as your other annual operating expenses. Since income is frequently in short supply, many organizations plan to fund only part of their annual budgeted depreciation expense to correspond with available income.

This is an especially good tip if you are budgeting depreciation for the first time. The more gradually you phase in funding expectations of depreciation expense, the less pinch you'll feel on the income side of the budget.

If you don't conduct an outside audit, use your own judgement plus the expertise of qualified board members in budgeting annual depreciation expense levels.

If you do have an outside audit, your flexibility in determining annual depreciation expense will usually be limited to the assumptions you make in setting your organization's capital asset depreciation schedule (the number of years of useful life consistently assigned to each asset type, for example). Remember, your auditor will include the full amount of scheduled depreciation as expense in your annual audited financial statements. So the amount of depreciation expense not funded by income will eat into your planned year-end surplus and could even generate an operating deficit.

Managing Reserve Funds

Nonprofits tend to use reserves in three primary ways:

1. As *working capital* to internally finance untimely receipt of accounts receivable or to support rapid organizational growth,

2. As *repair and replacement reserves* to repair or acquire fixed assets over time (see Capital Budgets in Chapter 2), and

3. As *venture capital reserves* to provide seed capital for self-funded new programs.

No matter what the eventual use of the reserve, though, we recommend the following reserve management strategies:

• Segregate reserve funds from the organization's general checking or savings accounts to resist the tendency to spend the reserve on routine operating expenses.

• Make sure the board and other senior managers know what the reserves are for so there is no tendency to spend for operating purposes.

• If appropriate, name the reserve account in accordance with its purpose.

• List your reserve funds in separate categories on your internal financial statements and annual audit. Technically they are part of your organization's cash and *unrestricted* net assets. But nonprofits frequently find it easier to remember their purpose when segregated from general savings. (Refer back to Figure 16: Sample Balance Sheet and Income Statement on page 91.)

The Board's Role in Monitoring Reserve Funds

Setting policies for the use of reserve funds falls within the board of directors' role. Board-developed fiscal policies not only assure prudent use of reserves, they also provide a good practice ground to demonstrate sound fiscal policies to outside funders on the organization's ability to manage and preserve excess cash.

In addition to the board fiscal policies outlined in Chapter 3, it is critical that the board:

• Understand the purpose of the reserve fund and how and why it was established,
• Be committed to its effective use, and
• Set policies which authorize how and when draws will be made and repaid.

Cash reserves are an important stabilizing element for dynamic, growing nonprofits. They provide an internal source of working capital every mid-size organization needs to run a financially smooth operation.

There is certainly more that could be said about cash reserves. Indeed, although this chapter was not meant to be a full articulation of the philosophy, use, or management of reserves, it nonetheless again makes the central point of this book: The budget, when strategically and properly prepared, can contribute greatly to your nonprofit organization's financial health and sustainability.

Summary

So there you have it—everything you need to know about how to prepare a nonprofit budget, and how to use it to your fullest advantage.

We hope you've found in this book what we meant to provide. Tips on:

- How to approach budgeting
- What type of budget will work best for your organization
- How to adopt an *income-based* approach to budgeting
- How to better understand and fund your indirect costs
- How to segregate your program costs from one another
- How to use the budget to set pricing and develop unit costs
- How to use the budget to establish cash reserves

We wish you the greatest success as you make the most of every opportunity within the realistic framework of your nonprofit budget.

Glossary of
Selected Terms

Glossary of Selected Terms

Balanced budget	A budget in which projected expenditures for a given period are matched by expected revenues for the same period.
Budget	A financial plan that estimates the monetary receipts and expenditures for an operating period. Budgets may be directed toward project or program activities and are primarily used as a comparison and control feature against the actual financial results.
Budget-based spending	A practice of spending according to an approved expense budget, without taking into consideration any changes that may occur in the actual revenue received by the organization.
Capital budget	A budget that includes capital outlays and the means of financing them for the current fiscal year.
Capital purchase	Assets, such as land, buildings, furniture, and equipment, that require their own budget and financial treatment.
Conditional promise to give	A written or oral agreement to contribute cash or other assets to your organization in which the contribution depends on the occurrence of a specified future uncertain event to bind the promisor.
Deficit	1. Expenses and losses in excess of related income; an operating loss. 2. An accumulation of operating losses ("negative" retained income).
Depreciation	A non-cash charge to expense which reflects the declining value of a fixed asset.
Direct expense	An expense that can be applied specifically (but not necessarily exclusively) to a certain activity.
Expense	An asset expended resulting in a decrease in net assets.

FASB	See *Financial Accounting Standards Board.*
Financial Accounting Standards Board	The Financial Accounting Standards Board (FASB) is the governing board that formulates authoritative accounting standards for nongovernmental agencies. These standards, which encompass accounting rules, procedures, and applications, define accepted accounting practice and are referred to as Generally Accepted Accounting Principles (GAAP).
Fiscal policies	Specific accounting principles and methods employed by an organization that are considered the most appropriate to ensure proper internal controls are in place and that financial reports produced are in accordance with generally accepted accounting principles.
Fiscal year	The 12-month period of time to which the annual budget applies and at the end of which the organization determines its financial position and the results of its operations.
Fixed costs	Operating costs that do not change from year to year nor vary with an increase or decrease in activity.
Functional-based budget	See *program-based budget.*
GAAP	See *Generally Accepted Accounting Principles.*
Generally Accepted Accounting Principles	Accounting standards for nongovernmental agencies that encompass accounting rules, procedures, and applications, and define accepted accounting practice. See also *FASB.*
Income-based budget	A budget process that begins with realistic income projections and then goes on to determine realistic costs for next year's service delivery.

Income-based spending   A practice of spending according to actual, rather than budgeted, income. It correlates to income-based budgeting.

Income released from restrictions   Temporarily restricted income received in a prior period that can now be spent.

Indirect expense   An expense that benefits multiple programs and cannot be directly assigned specifically to one program or another. Examples include audit and accounting fees, general liability or directors and officers liability insurance, and general marketing expenses.

Line-item budget   A method of presenting an overall categorical picture of an agency's income and expense items. It gives an at-a-glance look at what expected income and expenses will be for a given period.

Operating budget   A budget that applies to all receipts and expenditures other than capital outlays.

Operating deficit   A deficit that results from an excess of expenses and losses over related income during an accounting period.

Operating reserve   A reserve designated for cash operating purposes (see *reserve*).

Operating surplus   A surplus that results from an excess of income over related expenses and losses during an accounting period.

Permanently restricted net assets   A donor-imposed restriction that stipulates contributed assets be maintained permanently. Unless otherwise stipulated by the donor or state law, the organization is permitted to use up or expend part or all of the income derived from permanently restricted assets.

Program-based budget	A budget that isolates the activities of individual programs from one another and segregates program expenses from administrative or fundraising costs. Also called a "functional" or "activity" budget.
Repair and replacement reserve	A reserve designated for fixed asset repair and replacement (see *reserve*).
Reserve	An account that segregates a portion of unrestricted net assets and related cash assets for some future use as designated by the board of directors.
Revenue	Assets earned or income from services performed or goods sold.
Support	Income from voluntary contributions and grants.
Surplus	Support and revenue in excess of expenses.
Temporarily restricted net assets	A donor-imposed restriction on contributed assets which will eventually either expire with the passage of time or will be fulfilled through action by the organization.
Unit costs	A term used in cost accounting to denote the cost of producing a unit of product or rendering a unit of service.
Unrestricted net assets	Sometimes called operating funds or general funds, this net asset group contains the assets on which there are no donor restrictions and from which the bulk of financial activity is usually handled.
Variable costs	Operating costs that fluctuate in direct proportion to the changes in activity.
Variance	Difference between expenses and income projected on the budget and actual results of financial activity.

Appendix of Worksheets

- Worksheet 1: Income Projection Worksheet
- Worksheet 2: Statement of Revenue and Expense with Budget Comparisons
- Worksheet 3: Identifying Your Programs
- Worksheet 4: Program-Based Budget
- Worksheet 5: Functional Time Estimate
- Worksheet 6: Periodic Time Report
- Worksheet 7: Daily Time Report
- Worksheet 8: Salary Expenses

	Projection to Current Year-End	Proposed Budget	Certain	Reasonably Certain	Uncertain/ Possible	Total
SUPPORT						
Government Grants						
1.	$	$	$	$	$	$
2.						
3.						
Foundation Grants						
1.						
2.						
3.						
4.						
5.						
6.						
7.						
8.						
Individual Contributions						
In-Kind Support						
Other						
1.						
2.						
3.						
REVENUE						
Contracts						
1.						
2.						
3.						
Earned Income						
1.						
2.						
3.						
Membership Fee						
Interest						
Total Support & Revenue	$	$	$	$	$	$

Statement of Revenue and Expense with Budget Comparisons
For the Period Ended _____, _____

	Current Month			Year To-Date			Annual Budget
	Actual	Budget	Variance	Actual	Budget	Variance	
Income							
Grants	$	$	$	$	$	$	$
Government Contracts							
Fees							
Interest							
Miscellaneous							
Total Income	$	$	$	$	$	$	$
Expenses							
Salaries	$	$	$	$	$	$	$
Payroll Taxes							
Health Benefits							
Other Benefits							
Total Personnel Expenses							
Audit/Acct. Fees							
Equipment Lease							
Insurance							
Training/Education – Staff							
Promotional Expenses							
Consultant Fees							
Program Activities							
Supplies							
Office Equip./Repair							
Postage							
Telephone							
Occupancy							
Public Relations							
Utilities							
Depreciation							
Other Supplies							
Total Direct Expense before Indirect Allocation							
Indirect Allocation							
Total Expenses	$	$	$	$	$	$	$
Excess Surplus/(Deficit)							

Your Organization: _____

Your Programs:

1. _____

2. _____

3. _____

4. _____

5. _____

6. _____

7. _____

8. _____

9. Fundraising _____

10. Administrative _____

Program-Based Budget

For the Period Ended _____, _____

		A	B	C	D	E	F
							Indirect
		Total	Program 1	Program 2	Program 3	Fundraising	Administrative
	Income						
1.	Grants	$	$	$	$	$	$
2.	Government Contracts						
3.	Fees						
4.	Interest						
5.	Miscellaneous						
6.	Total Income	$	$	$	$	$	$
	Expenses						
7.	Salaries	$	$	$	$	$	$
8.	Payroll Taxes						
9.	Health Benefits						
10.	Other Benefits						
11.	Total Personnel Expenses						
12.	Audit/Acct. Fees						
13.	Equipment Lease						
14.	Insurance						
15.	Training/Education – Staff						
16.	Promotional Expenses						
17.	Consultant Fees						
18.	Program Activities						
19.	Supplies						
20.	Office Equip./Repair						
21.	Postage						
22.	Telephone						
23.	Occupancy						
24.	Public Relations						
25.	Utilities						
26.	Depreciation						
27.	Other Supplies						
28.	**Total Direct Expenses before Indirect Allocation**						
29.	**Indirect Allocation**						
30.	**Total Expenses**						
31.	**Excess Surplus/(Deficit)**	$	$	$	$	$	$

Staff Name and Position   _____

_____   Program 1

_____   Program 2

_____   Program 3

_____   Fundraising

_____   Administrative

_____100%_____   Total

Staff Name and Position _____

Week Beginning _____, _____

	Mon	Tues	Wed	Thur	Fri	Sat	Sun	Total
Program 1	_____	_____	_____	_____	_____	_____	_____	_____
Program 2	_____	_____	_____	_____	_____	_____	_____	_____
Program 3	_____	_____	_____	_____	_____	_____	_____	_____
Fundraising	_____	_____	_____	_____	_____	_____	_____	_____
Administrative	_____	_____	_____	_____	_____	_____	_____	_____
Total	_____	_____	_____	_____	_____	_____	_____	_____

Staff Name _____   **Month** _____, _____

DATE:	1	2	3	4	5	6	7	8	9	10	11	12	13	14	15		
	16	17	18	19	20	21	22	23	24	25	26	27	28	29	30	31	TOTAL
Program 1																	
Program 2																	
Program 3																	
Fundraising																	
Administrative																	
Sick																	
Vacation																	
Holiday																	
TOTAL																	

Worksheet 8: Salary Expenses

	A		B		C		D		Indirect E		F	
	Total		Program 1		Program 2		Program 3		Fundraising		Administrative	
Position	Percent	Dollars	Percent	Dollars	Percent	Dollars	Percent	Dollars	Percent	Dollars	Percent	Dollars
1.	100%	$	%	$	%	$	%	$	%	$	%	$
2.	100%	$	%	$	%	$	%	$	%	$	%	$
3.	100%	$	%	$	%	$	%	$	%	$	%	$
4.	100%	$	%	$	%	$	%	$	%	$	%	$
5.	100%	$	%	$	%	$	%	$	%	$	%	$
6.	100%	$	%	$	%	$	%	$	%	$	%	$
7.	100%	$	%	$	%	$	%	$	%	$	%	$
8.	100%	$	%	$	%	$	%	$	%	$	%	$
9.	100%	$	%	$	%	$	%	$	%	$	%	$
10.	100%	$	%	$	%	$	%	$	%	$	%	$
11.	100%	$	%	$	%	$	%	$	%	$	%	$
12.	100%	$	%	$	%	$	%	$	%	$	%	$
13. TOTAL	100%	$	%	$	%	$	%	$	%	$	%	$

Index

Index

A

Allocation methods, 68

B

Board's role in budget, 30
Board's role in monitoring reserves, 93
Budget, purpose of, 9
Budget steps, 26
Budget timeline, 27
Budget-based spending, 10
Budgeting an operating surplus, 33
Budgeting for reserves, 90

C

Capital budget, 22
Conditional promises to give, 39

D

Deficit, 35
Depreciation, 88
Direct expense, 47, 67

E

Expenses, 46

F

Fiscal policies, 31
Fixed costs, 46
Functional allocation methods, 66

I

Income-based budget, 17, 28
Income-based spending, 10
Income projection worksheet, 29
    example of, 21
Income released from restriction, 41
Indirect expense, 47, 67
Indirect expense allocation methods, 68

L

Line-item budget, 14
    example of, 15

M

Management's role in budget, 32
Managing reserves, 92

O

Overhead, 46

P

Permanently restricted net assets, 41
Personnel expense allocation, 55
Personnel time records, 57
Pricing, 82
Program-based budget, 16, 52
    example of, 18

R

Repair and replacement reserve, 88
Reserves, 88
Restricted income, 40

S

Surplus, 33, 88

T

Temporarily restricted net assets, 41

U

Unit costs, 81
Unrestricted net assets, 40

V

Variable costs, 46
Variance, 28, 35

About the Authors

LarsonAllen Public Service Group provides consulting, training, and accounting services to nonprofits, foundations, educational institutions, and government entities. It was created through the merger of The Stevens Group, a consulting and training firm for nonprofits and foundations, and the nonprofit and government divisions of Larson, Allen, Weishair & Co., LLP, a diversified professional service firm. LarsonAllen Public Service Group now represents a team of highly skilled professionals with experience and professional degrees in accounting, business, finance, law, public affairs, social services, and the arts.

Debra L. Ruegg, a principal and senior consultant in LarsonAllen Public Service Group, joined the firm in 1990 and has since worked extensively with foundations and nonprofits on financial and organizational assessments and system design. Debra is the co-author of a book on bookkeeping basics published by the Amherst H. Wilder Foundation Publishing Center in 2002 as well as an experienced and popular trainer in the area of financial management and techniques.

Terry M. Fraser, CPA, a principal in LarsonAllen Public Service Group, has worked extensively with the nonprofit community for over 20 years, primarily in the charitable organization arena. She served as one of fifteen on the AICPA Not-for-Profit Committee that wrote the current accounting and audit guide for nonprofits. Terry also has significant experience in dealing with audit compliance issues and the wide variety of challenges faced by the nonprofit industry.

Anne L. Howden, a senior consultant in LarsonAllen Public Service Group, joined the firm in 1994. In addition to her consulting work with foundations and nonprofits around the country, Anne is a national lecturer, public speaker, and trainer on a variety of financial and organizational management topics, including budgeting. During her 20-year career, Anne has served in senior financial and administrative roles for major Twin Cities nonprofit social service, arts, and funding organizations.

Susan Kenny Stevens leads the Public Service Group, having founded The Stevens Group in 1982 and merged it into LarsonAllen in 1998. Susan is a consultant and advisor to numerous national and local foundations and has authored several articles, studies, and books on financial and management topics, most recently: *Nonprofit Lifecycles: Stage-based Wisdom for Nonprofit Capacity* (2001), *Investing in Capacity: How the Working Capital Fund Promotes Sustainable Change* (2001), *All the Way to the Bank: Smart Money Management for Tomorrow's Nonprofit* (1997), and *Keeping the Books: Developing Financial Capacity in Your Nonprofit Press* (1996).

CD Disclaimer

READ THIS: You should read the terms and conditions before opening the enclosed CD with this book. By opening the accompanying packet, you acknowledge that you have read and accept the following terms and conditions.

1. The worksheets included on this CD are constructed using Microsoft® Excel 97 (PC format). If you have different software or an older version of Excel you may not be able to open the spreadsheets. You will need a basic understanding of spreadsheet software to use the worksheets.

2. The formulas built into the worksheets are for the specific number of columns and rows as demonstrated on hard copies of the worksheets found in the appendix of the text. If you alter the number of columns and/or rows you need to adjust the formulas accordingly to maintain accuracy.

3. Larson, Allen, Weishair & Co., LLP's ("LarsonAllen") entire liability and your exclusive remedy for defects in materials and workmanship shall be limited to replacement of the CD, which may be returned to LarsonAllen with a copy of your receipt at the following address: LarsonAllen, 220 South Sixth Street, Suite 300, Minneapolis, MN 55402. This limited warranty is void if failure of the worksheets has resulted from accident, abuse, or misapplication.

4. In no event shall LarsonAllen or the authors be liable for any damages whatsoever from the use of the worksheets.